going places

East Anglia & Essex

Cambridgeshire
Essex
Norfolk
Suffolk

Titles in this Series

RAC going places

East Anglia & Essex

Cambridgeshire
Essex
Norfolk
Suffolk

K D Clark

The Publishing Division of
The Royal Automobile Club
83-85 Pall Mall   London

First published 1981

An RAC publication

The twelve tour commentaries and accompanying maps in this book have been chosen, planned and written by the author and not by the RAC.

ISBN 0 86211 009 2

Cover picture: The Ancient House, Ipswich

Designed and produced for the RAC by
Walter Oliver Publishing Services
Illustrations by Ed Perera
Typeset by Print Things Ltd
Printed and bound by Ebenezer Baylis & Son Limited
The Trinity Press, Worcester, and London

Made and printed in Great Britain

Contents

The National Trust

There are hundreds of places of outstanding artistic and archeological interest in the 'RAC Going Places' series which are under the care of the National Trust. If you write to them at 42 Queen Anne's Gate, London SW1 you can get full information on how to join and thereby save a considerable sum in entry fees to their properties

Acknowledgements

Many people and organizations have assisted in the preparation of this book, but the author is particularly grateful for the willing help given by the staffs of the East Anglia Tourist Board, the Norfolk Museum Service and the Forestry Commission

Introduction

East Anglia and Essex are flat, people say. It would be more accurate to say that there are no high hills. But the area has lots of compensating attractions: an abundance of medieval architecture unsurpassed in any other part of Britain, and including the great cathedrals of Norwich and Ely, Cambridge's ancient colleges, hundreds of Tudor cottages, churches between five hundred and eight hundred years old, many historic houses with attractive gardens open to the public, and the second biggest English forest – at Thetford. And nowhere in East Anglia and Essex are you further than 50 miles from near-deserted beaches, so that each day you can choose between the countryside and the seaside – and in fact you may often enjoy both!

Topography

East Anglia and Essex may be divided into three main zones topographically – a central clay belt flanked by two areas of lighter soils and these three zones can be further sub-divided on the basis of their varying soils and vegetation.

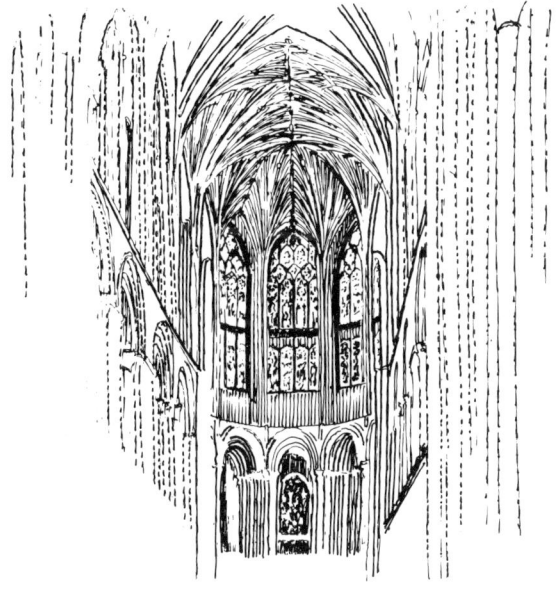

Interior of the Choir, Norwich Cathedral

Chalk to a great depth (betraying its oceanic origin) under-
lies much of East Anglia – it is the end of a range that forms the
Berkshire downs, stretching through Hertfordshire and Cambridgeshire, where it forms the Gog Magog hills. In Norfolk it
gives character to the country in the area bounded by Hock-
wold to Diss in the south, Hunstanton in the east and Blakeney
in the north; most of Norfolk's rivers rise in this area. The chalk
is covered by strata of sand (particularly in the Thetford area),
gravel or clay. In the east of Norfolk and Suffolk the chalk is
overlaid with Norwich crag and Chillesford clay to such a depth
that the chalk is not visible even in the seaside cliffs. In
Cambridgeshire, Fenland overlies Jurassic clays and in the
southwest of the county the underlying chalk is edged by greensand and gault clay.

Stone is non-existent in most of East Anglia and Essex but
up in the northwest of Norfolk a dark brown stone called
carstone is found – you may see it in Sandringham's parish
church. Flint is plentiful in the chalk and it is found everywhere
in churches and houses, and in public buildings such as the
great Guildhall at King's Lynn. (A visit to a flint mine near
Thetford is included in Tour 9.)

The greater part of southern Essex lies on London clay – the
chalk is evident in the north but then lies very deeply until it
surfaces again around Purfleet and Grays Thurrock. Boulder
clay (a lighter looking clay and easier to drain than London
clay) is found in the region of Essex northwest of the A12
between Marks Tey and Ingatestone.

Rivers

The river system of Norfolk is intriguing: the majority of the
rivers flow either east or west, reaching the sea at King's Lynn
and Great Yarmouth respectively. But East Anglian rivers
seem reluctant to reach the sea and have meandering courses.

The main east-flowing rivers are the Ant, Thurne, Bure,
Yare and Waveney. The Ant rises (appropriately) near
Antingham and flows into Barton Broad and then joins the
Bure east of Horning. The Thurne has a strange course, rising
near the coast north of Sea Palling eventually passing through
Hickling Broad and Heigham Sound and joining the Bure near
the village of Thurne. The Bure begins near Melton Constable
reaching Coltishall and the Broads, flowing through Wroxham;
after Horning it is joined by the Ant and Thurne and flows into
Breydon Water at the back of Great Yarmouth. The Yare also
flows into Breydon – it rises east of Shipdham and flows south
of Norwich and the Wensum flows into it – it then takes a huge
south north loop (all navigable and a popular sailing river)

receiving the Waveney before reaching Breydon, as mentioned. The Waveney is important because it forms the boundary with Suffolk from its source to its mouth; it rises near South Lopham (where the Little Ouse also begins but flows in the opposite direction), flows round Bungay, almost reaches Lowestoft but then takes a great loop northwards, joining the . Yare at Bredon Water.

The Little Ouse is the main westward flowing river of Norfolk. After South Lopham it runs into Thetford, where the Thet flows into it, it reaches Fenland, where Cambridgeshire is on its left bank instead of Suffolk, is joined by the Ouse, the two together then being called the Great Ouse, reaching King's Lynn and the Wash.

The rivers of Suffolk and Essex are not so complex. The famous Stour rises in Cambridgeshire and enters Suffolk north of Haverhill; it then forms the boundary between Suffolk and Essex and continues to do so until it reaches Harwich. The Alde starts its life north of Dennington and almost reaches the sea at Aldeburgh but instead takes a sweep southwards and joins the Ore before reaching the sea. The Orwell is called the Gipping after its birthplace but becomes the Orwell after refreshing Ipswich. The Deben rises at Debenham flowing south to Woodbridge where it becomes a wide estuary down to Felixstowe. In Essex the Colne rises near Birdbrook and passes Castle Hedingham, Halstead and through the Colne valley to Colchester, forming a wide estuary and encircling Mersea Island. The Blackwater river also reaches the sea in the same area, starting south of Saffron Walden, passing Braintree, being joined by the Chelmer and becoming an estuary of Maldon. The river Stort forms the eastern boundary of Essex from Bishop's Stortford to Roydon, where it becomes the Lea passing Waltham Abbey and Chingford.

Cambridgeshire has few rivers flowing in a natural fashion as the flat Fen country lies mostly in the county and its waters have been regulated into drains and dykes. (See under Fenland in the Places of Interest section.) The main rivers are the Great Ouse, which enters the county from the west at Earith (and is diverted into the Old and New Bedford rivers), the Cam, which flows through Cambridge from the north, and the Nene, which crosses the Isle of Ely from Peterborough and flows through Wisbech (most picturesquely) to the sea.

Apart from the Fens, the two other areas of special interest in East Anglia and Essex are the Broads and Breckland. Broadland stretches roughly from east of a line from Mundesley to Norwich and north of a line from Norwich to Yarmouth. The waters of the Broads are some ten to twelve feet deep and it has been determined in recent years that this came about from the flooding of areas where peat-digging took place between the 12th and 14th centuries. These great stretches of water remained isolated and undisturbed until the 19th-century enthusiasm for sailing and the 20th-century madness for motor cruising brought a great holiday industry to the area. Boat-building and other activities associated with the holiday industry were developed, transforming the almost nonexistent economy of this region. (See under Broadland.)

Finally there is one of the most fascinating areas – Breckland (Tour 9) – some 400 square miles stretching from Narborough in the north and East Harling in the east, to Stoke Ferry and Lakenheath in the west. Once called the East Anglian desert, Breckland was formerly a dry area of windblown sand. Before afforestation the wind caused large rolling dunes and in the 17th century the diarist John Evelyn recommended the planting of trees as the only means of holding the soils of this area – and how right he was. It is thought now that Breckland was not always so infertile and that over-grazing by sheep in the Middle Ages destroyed the shallow-rooted vegetation which once existed there.

An unusual fact about Breckland is that its name was invented by a young writer, W G Clarke, author of *In Breckland Wilds*. After its publication in 1925 he went on to become a great Norfolk naturalist. A large part of the area was transformed by the planting, by the Forestry Commission, of 80 square miles of Scots and Corsican pines in the 1920's, creating Thetford Forest. Although some people criticize the dullness of pine forests. Thetford Forest affords many attractions for visitors and these are described later.

In the foregoing sketch of the general geography of East Anglia the coastline has been thought of as being in its present position. But it was not always so. About 6 000 BC East Anglia was still joined to Europe, the coastline stretching from Yorkshire round the Dogger Bank and reaching Jutland. In the post-glacial period the ice sheets covering the land melted, creating what is now the North Sea (and incidentally causing the land to rise slowly, but not evenly). Evidence of this change persists in that the trunks of ancient trees can still be seen at very low tides off the Norfolk coast at Thornham and Titchwell.

Flora and Fauna

The wild flora of East Anglia is interesting and varied. Apart from the unique Breckland area (see under Thetford Forest in Places of Interest) there are the Broads, (which support fens and reedswamps and flora not found elsewhere in Britain), the coast dunes and salt-marshes, the greensand heaths and chalk uplands, all with their own special plant life.

The saltmarsh plants include sea lavender, sea aster, sea purslane, and thrift. Along the marsh walls sea beet, shore and sea wormwood grow. The mudflats support marsh samphires, sea-blite and rice-grass; the latter has raised the level of great areas of tidal mud in recent years. And on the beach shingle banks you may see the sea-pea, with its bright green foliage and bright purple flowers, also the yellow horned-poppy, sea campion, curled dock, sea sandwort, biting stonecrop (that sounds dangerous!) and sticky groundsel.

The heathland of sand and gravels supports heather, bracken and gorse. You will also find harebells, heath bed-straw, tormentil and sheep's sorrel. A particularly bright red plant, mossy tillaea, a sort of dwarf stonecrop should make itself visible on the heath.

Because East Anglia enjoys a generally dry climate and is well drained, there are not so many areas where true bog plants grow. However, there are a few, generally in valleys near the source of streams. There you will find the marsh gentian, butterwort, bog asphodel, and white beaksedge.

The more common plants such as the wood anemone, primrose, bluebell, lesser celandine, violets, wood sorrel and red campion will be found in woodland areas of clay in central and south Norfolk and Suffolk. Rarer species of those areas are Herb Paris, cow-wheat, the greater butterfly orchid, woodruff and lily of the valley, and even rarer, creeping lady's tresses (thought to have come from Scotland with the introduction of pine trees) is only found in woods near Holt.

East Anglian woods produce toadstools in great variety in rainy seasons. The notorious death-cap is commoner here than in any other part of Britain and is generally found in oakwoods. Another toadstool to be found is the quaint earth star, which flourishes in great abundance and variety. Remember though that toadstools are to be seen, not eaten!

As regards animal life, the general observer will notice that the red squirrel occurs in East Anglia although it is rare else-where in Britain. (The grey squirrel is creeping in as well.) Another phenomenon of East Anglia has been the coypu, a cat-sized amphibious rodent originating in South America. The coypu spread alarmingly along the waterways of east Nor-folk in the 1950's after some of the animals escaped from a fur farm near Norwich. The coypu is destructive of river banks and a concerted campaign in the late 1950's and early 1960's did much to control the pest – the severe winter of 1963 also did much to help. But isolated colonies of the animal still persist, particularly in the Breckland meres.

Afforestation has much changed birdlife throughout East Anglia. Big increases have occurred in the populations of titmice, thrushes, blackbirds and woodpeckers. There are some crossbills in the forests (they like pine cones), but they are elusive birds. At the forest edges, redstarts and red-backed shrikes may be observed. There and on adjoining heathland the nightjar may be heard if not seen from May to August; you may also hear and see curlews. The great bustard was once a common bird in Breckland before the planting of trees; now it is a rare visitor to this country. The Breckland meres attract many water-birds and they are the main breeding centre for a particular breed of duck, the gadwall.

There are famous nature reserves at Minsmere and Havergate Island on the east Suffolk coast. At the former, rare breeding birds include the bearded tit, the bittern and marsh harrier. Avocets nest at Havergate and a spectacular colony of these long-legged black and white waders with upturned bills has become established there, under the care of the Royal Society for the Protection of Birds. Other species to be seen along the coast are shelduck, the little ringed plover, the hen harrier, the rough-legged buzzard, snow buntings and shore-larks (the last four are winter visitors).

The rivers of East Anglia are well stocked with coarse fish: pike, perch, roach, rudd and bream may be caught. Upper reaches of rivers are inhabited by dace, gudgeon, stone loach, ruffe, bullhead and minnow, while brown trout, rainbow trout and grayling have been introduced to provide sport. The chub is indigenous to the west-flowing rivers (Ouse, Wissey and Thet), but not to those flowing eastwards. And tench abound in lakes and meres.

Forestry

It is possible, if you visit the coastal areas, to get the impression of East Anglia and Essex as a flat countryside with very few trees. That was in fact the situation sixty years ago. But now East Anglia has a considerable acreage of forests, the major one at Thetford being the second largest in England. East Anglia's other forests, all under the enlightened eye of the Forestry Commission, are at Aldewood, between Ipswich and Aldeburgh, and at Lynn and Wensum, to the northeast of King's Lynn. Detailed descriptions of the many facilities available at these forests are shown under the entries for
Aldewood, Epping, Lynn and Wensum, and Thetford.

The major objective of the Forestry Commission is to grow timber on a commercial basis, but the Commission has long realised that their forests offer considerable opportunities for countryside recreation (they cover over two million acres in Britain) and have progressively provided more and more car parks, picnic and camping facilities, forest walks and trails, with information centres at the larger forests. Most forest walks, which are waymarked with coloured discs, start from car parks or picnic sites and are generally from two to three miles long. (If you wish to have more information there are free pamphlets available from the Forestry Commission at 231 Corstophine Road, Edinburgh EH12 7AT, both on the Forests of Southern England and Forestry Commission Camping and Caravan Sites.)

History

Early Settlers

Little is known of man in East Anglia in the Mesolithic Age (from 8 000 to 3 500 BC) partly because any timber structures have long-since disappeared and there is no natural stone which could be used for buildings similar to the ancient granite huts on Dartmoor. But this lack of stone brought about the building of the lovely timber houses which are still the pride of East Anglia. All we know about that time is that mixed oak woodlands were growing and that areas like Breckland were the home of wild boar, aurochs (a sort of wild ox) and of red and roe deer.

Evidence of the later Neolithic (or New Stone) Age, dating from 3 500 BC can be seen, and quite dramatically. The primitive farmers of that time began to clear the forests and their axes were made from mining the black flint of East Anglia. At Grime's Graves, near Weeting (Tour 9) you may see some of the 400 mines in that area (now in the charge of the Department of the Environment) and there is at least one deep mine which you may visit and see how the miners of 4 000 years ago sunk deep shafts and then dug lateral galleries. One of the mines was found to house a shrine – it contained a chalk figure carved in the image of a goddess of fertility and was left sur-rounded by a huge pile of the deer-horn picks which the miners used. This ancient industry still exists today in that flint-knapping continues as a local industry at nearby Brandon. The modern flints are used to make gun flints, still popular with Wild West clubs in America. The Bronze Age, from 1 800 to 700 BC saw the arrival of many new peoples from Germany and elsewhere, and the development of farming. But the bronze tools and ornaments discovered from that time were all

13

imported, because East Anglia had no copper and tin from which the alloy is made.

The Roman Age

The Romans occupied Britain for the 400 years from AD 43-410. And for information about the warring tribes then occupying East Anglia we can read the Commentaries of Julius Caesar himself, who invaded Britain in the years 55 and 54 BC. At that time there were two dominant tribes in East Anglia: the Iceni, a warrior tribe of French origin (later to be led by the famous Boudicca) who controlled all Norfolk and northwest Suffolk, and the Trinovantes, who held south eastern Suffolk.

Yet another and bigger tribe, the Catuvellauni, whose king was Cunobelinus (Shakespeare's Cymbeline) controlled a huge kingdom with its capital at Colchester (Tour 3), then called Camulodunum. The Iceni were being pressed northwards by the Catuvellauni and it is thought that the defensive earthworks at Thetford Castle (Tour 9) were built by the Iceni. But the Roman invasion by Claudius in AD 43 gave some respite to the Iceni at first – the Catuvellauni territory (including Colchester of course) was captured by the Romans, who wisely treated the fierce Iceni as a client kingdom for some twenty years. Roman rapacity was the cause of Boudicca's revolt in AD 60: at her husband's death only half of his wealth was bequeathed to the Emperor Nero. The Romans invaded Iceni territory, enslaving the tribal aristocracy and flogging Boudicca. While the main Roman army was at Lincoln and Anglesey the enraged Boudicca and her new allies the Trinovantes descended on Colchester, held by only 200 Romans. They were slaughtered, the worst massacres taking place in the great Roman Temple of Claudius in Colchester – you may still see the vaults of this temple beneath the Norman castle which now houses Colchester's museum. Boudicca swept on and sacked London.

But retribution was inevitable and when the Roman army reached the rebels their short swords and the lances of their cavalry made an overwhelming victory inevitable. Boudicca escaped to die of sickness, or some say by poison. The victorious Romans laid waste to the whole of East Anglia – many of the Iceni then buried their treasures and these hoards remained undiscovered for hundreds of years. Some of the Iceni and their allies were then deported to Fenland to work on drainage schemes to create new farmland for the Romans.

Two hundred years of peace ensued while the Romans established their civilizing administration. The areas they controlled were divided into units similar to our counties; that in the northern part of East Anglia was at Caistor-by-Norwich,

14

which the Romans called Venta Icenorum to show its relation to the old Iceni territory. Later the Romans built a chain of forts around the coast from the Wash as far as Hampshire to withstand Saxon invaders from the Continent. The most well-preserved is at Burgh Castle (Tour 6) built to guard the estuary of the Yare, Bure and Waveney rivers. A little further north-wards they established Caister-by-Yarmouth (Tour 6), a town and a port with a short sea-route to the Rhine. Caistor-by-Norwich was a sophisticated town, with a forum (market place), a basilica (town hall) with a colonnaded façade, and public baths; its population is thought to have been about a thousand.

The Romans rebuilt Colchester, the Roman province's political capital – the earlier city now being under the houses and roads of the outskirts of the modern town. Parts of the Roman town wall remain, but the most spectacular relic is the huge Balkerne Gateway. The Romans also drained part of the Fens: Car Dyke, of which some lengths remain, was a drainage channel as well as a means of communication between Cambridgeshire and Northamptonshire. Life was indeed becoming civilized under the Romans, as remains of Roman villas show. But after their departure in 410, grass began to grow over the ruins on towns, forts and country mansions, and farms were abandoned – the Dark Ages had arrived.

Saxons and Danes

The term 'Dark Ages' referring to the period following the departure of the Romans and before the Norman Conquest of 1066 implies that during that period life became less civilized and that it was an unhappy time of a series of invasions by warring tribes. Ironically it could also mean that we are 'in the dark' about that age, because there are scarcely any contemporary records – it was not until monastic writers such as Bede began their work that we have true records and there was much guesswork then about the unrecorded time. All we have is archaeological evidence and this, as the late R R Clarke wrote in his excellent *East Anglia* book about Ancient Peoples, 'tells us little about the living and much about the dead'. All we have found from the 5th century in East Anglia and Essex is a series of defensive ditches built to protect the Angles from the men of Wessex and Mercia – the most impressive being the eight-mile long Devil's Dyke stretching along the boundary of New-market Heath in Cambridgeshire.

By the 6th century a royal family of Scandinavian origin had conquered most of East Anglia, establishing its headquarters at Rendelsham and the royal burial ground at nearby Sutton Hoo

15

(Tour 2). There are ten barrows at Sutton Hoo and it was the excavation of one of these in 1939 which revealed dramatically the wealth of these seagoing peoples. The find has been described as 'the most significant as it is certainly the most splendid archaeological discovery ever made in the British Isles'. Although no human remains were found in the barrow, it has been established that it honoured a king of the Swedish Wuffa dynasty and that it was erected in the period 650-670. The fantastic treasure accompanying the burial is now exhibited at the British Museum, but there are copies of some of the items at the Ipswich Museum (Tour 1).

The Wuffing dynasty came to an end about 740. East Anglia remained a separate kingdom, but mainly as a vassal state owing allegiance to Mercia and later to Wessex. During this time, Christianity had spread to East Anglia and many of the local monarchs fostered the new faith. The seat of the first bishopric was probably established at Dunwich on the Suffolk coast. Later, because the see was so large, a separate bishopric was made at North Elmham, covering Norfolk. This was later moved to Norwich. Many monasteries were known to have been founded in other parts of East Anglia at this time, but there is little trace of them now.

It should be added that, in Saxon times, the Bishop of London was also the Bishop of Essex. This had begun during the time when Essex was administered from St Albans, lasting until 1914 when Chelmsford became the ecclesiastical centre of the Essex diocese. (See Chelmsford.)

But there was to be no peace for these Christian centres. From 850 to 1066 East Anglia suffered from the ravages of the bloodthirsty Danes, first in a series of piratical raids and then in wars. In 869 the invaders established their winter headquarters at Thetford. In 870 the Danes captured King Edmund of the East Angles, had him tortured by the archers and then beheaded (see under Bury St Edmunds). The Danes' main enemy was Alfred the Great, then King of Wessex, who defeated them in 878, but allowed part of the Danish army to settle in East Anglia. Their settlements may still be identified by the surviving Danish place names – towns and villages ending in thorpe, toft, thwaite and by.

Despite this warlike activity, there was economic progress in East Anglia under the stimulus of close commercial contact with the Rhineland, so that by the eve of the Norman conquest townships sheltering considerable populations flourished at Norwich, Ipswich, Thetford, Dunwich, Bury St Edmunds, Colchester and Cambridge.

The Normans

Norman monuments in the shape of castles and ecclesiastical buildings abound in East Anglia and Essex. There are superb examples of Norman castles, and these are referred to under Castle Acre, Castle Rising, Colchester, Framlingham, Hedingham, Norwich, Orford and Thetford.

In the years immediately following the Conquest the Normans were in a potentially rebellious countryside and defensive castles had to be thrown up quickly. The most basic kind were the motte-and-bailey type, the motte being simply a huge mound of earth (or sometimes a natural feature) surrounded by an open space called a bailey, which in turn had a ditch or moat round it. The motte was defended by a wooden palisade. The mottes at Thetford (Tour 9), and at Chipping Ongar give a good idea of this simple kind of defence.

Stouter castles were built in the 12th century and it is interesting to learn that 'permission to crenellate' had to be sought from the king. You may see such an authority in a letter on show at Oxburgh Hall (Tour 9). Most castles were at the centre of a manorial system and the manors, or grants of land, were given by the king to his supporters in battle. In return for the land the lord of the manor was expected to provide the king with men for his army when needed. In Norfolk Roger Bigod received no less than 187 manors and William de Warenne 145 – some 500 others were distributed among other loyalists. In Suffolk the notorious Bishop Odo, brother of the Conqueror, was lord of many manors. (That did not mean that these men were always loyal to the king, as you will read under the entries for some of the castles mentioned above.) The Domesday Books, recorded in 1086, give an interesting insight into how manors and smaller parcels of land were distributed after the Norman Conquest. In many parts of East Anglia and Essex the 'middle men' retained their smallholdings by transferring their allegiance to their new Norman 'protectors'. A contrast between the proportion of free men to others in Suffolk and Essex set down in the Domesday Books is revealing: in Suffolk it was 40 per cent (amazingly more than half of all the free men in England then were in Suffolk), compared with the low percentage of seven per cent in Essex.

The Normans were also energetic builders of monasteries and churches. The remains of Castle Acre (Tour 8) will give you some idea of the huge scale of the monasteries. By 1200 there were over 80 monasteries in East Anglia, controlling vast estates, so that the church was important economically as well as spiritually. In fact the area of cultivated land was greatly increased in the early Middle Ages. Many new villages were founded and East Anglia and Essex became the most densely populated region of Britain.

There are few surviving Norman churches but the rare round churches built by the Knights Templars at Cambridge (Tour 12) and at Little Maplestead (Tour 3) are basically Norman. And of course Norwich Cathedral (Tours 5, 6 and 7), Ely Cathedral (Tour 10) and Waltham Abbey included stupendous examples of Norman work (albeit with many later additions).

The Middle Ages

Life in East Anglia in the early Middle Ages, with agriculture mainly controlled by the church, sounds peaceful enough. The countryside must have looked very different though, because there was not so much arable farming then – huge areas of land were devoted to the raising of sheep. However, the Barons were not a quiet breed, and were constantly fighting either each other or the King, see under Framlingham and Caister Castle. The most serious change came about with the Dissolution of the Monasteries in the 15th century. The monastic estates were often sold to ruthless 'new men' who frequently enclosed common land. This led to the peasants' rising in 1549, led by the Kett brothers of Wymondham (Tour 7). Kett led his men to Mousehold Heath, north of Norwich, where 20 000 people assembled. They captured Norwich and controlled much of the surrounding countryside. The first army sent by the King was defeated and Lord Sheffield was slain near the cathedral (a plaque marks the spot). A larger force quelled the revolt however, and terrible revenge was taken: William Kett was hanged alive from a tower of Wymondham Abbey and his brother Robert suffered a similar fate on the walls of Norwich castle (you may see the plaque erected there in 1949 by The Citizens of Norwich).

The 17th and 18th Centuries

East Anglia seems to have bred a great many 'fighters for freedom' because the following century brought forth the Huntingdon born Oliver Cromwell. During the Civil War most of the area was on the side of Parliament, except for towns such as King's Lynn and Colchester.

But the 17th century saw many quiet years in East Anglia. That was the time when the rich families such as the Boleyns and Wymondhams were building their great houses at Blickling Hall and Felbrigg Hall (Tour 5). As has been noted, Norfolk has no local stone and these mansions were masterpieces of brickbuilding. (An even greater achievement was in the build-

18

ing of Oxburgh Hall, also of brick, in the 15th century. That was built by the Bedingfield family in 1482 who (amazingly) are still in residence today.)

The 18th century saw the decline of the wool trade in East Anglia. It had brought about great wealth, which in turn influenced the building of comfortable houses and great churches in villages like Lavenham, Long Melford (Tour 11) and Saffron Walden. But the mechanization of weaving, needing power from water and coal, caused the weaving trade to flourish in the north of England.

East Anglia fell back on its basic industry, agriculture. Local landowners Coke of Norfolk (who lived at Holkham Hall (Tour 8) and Turnip Townshend of Raynham Hall, were pioneers in farming methods, and introduced new ways of rotating crops and of breeding cattle.

The 19th and 20th centuries

The Norfolk four-course crop rotation, with clover, wheat, fodder crops followed by barley, was practised all over East Anglia throughout the 19th and into the 20th century. The greatest revolution came with the introduction of the beet-sugar crop in the 1920's. East Anglia now grows a quarter of all the sugar beet grown in Britain. The old crop rotation is not generally followed now, since no fodder crops are needed because there are no sheep. However, in some areas a similar system still prevails because the sugar beet itself produces fodder in the form of crowns and pulp suitable for livestock feeding.

The coming of the railways probably brought about the most changes in East Anglia and Essex in the 19th century, transforming former fishing villages (such as Cromer) into flourishing holiday resorts. Changing leisure patterns also influenced the creation of Broadland as a centre for sailing holidays. But agriculture continues to be the main industry in East Anglia, which possesses in Fenland some of the richest soils in Britain. Southern Essex has become more industrialized of course (and during this century some of Essex has been lost to London). The most recent change has been a return to earlier times in the increase in shipping trade at ports such as King's Lynn, Yarmouth and Ipswich. As in those times the closeness of East Anglia and Essex to Europe is again influencing their way of life and her prosperity.

East Anglia's Artists

It is a phenomenon of the East Anglian countryside that it produced a plenitude of painters in the 18th and early 19th centuries. The Lake District had a similar group of writers at the same time but the others (Coleridge, Southey and later Ruskin) were drawn there by the native-born Wordsworth.

The East Anglian artists divide themselves into two groups: Gainsborough and Constable, who were born within ten miles of each other in the Ipswich area, the second group being the extraordinary family of painters including Crome, Cotman and Stannard who formed the Norwich School.

Thomas Gainsborough

Thomas Gainsborough was born in 1727, 50 years before Constable, at Sudbury (Tour 1). Educated at the Sudbury Grammar School, he showed early ability at painting and was sent to London as a pupil of a French engraver named Gravelot at the age of 14, returning to Sudbury at 19. There he announced his marriage to the natural daughter of the second Duke of Beaufort, who happily had an income of some £200 a year – worth some thousands in present-day money. The young couple set up home in Ipswich, where Gainsborough attracted some patrons and began portrait painting. It was said of him that 'he painted portraits to live and lived to paint landscapes'. In 1759 Gainsborough sold up his household goods and pictures somewhere opposite the Shire Hall at Ipswich and moved to fashionable Bath where many rich patrons lived, there becoming a most successful portrait painter. He later went to London and became the most fashionable painter in town. He died in 1788. Unlike other artists he never travelled abroad and although said to have been influenced first by Watteau and later by Rubens and Van Dyck he seems to have become a painter by instinct. His landscapes may now be considered stylistic and artificial. In this and his whole life he was a complete contrast with the boy born down the valley, John Constable.

John Constable

John Constable was born in 1776 at East Bergholt (Tour 1) one of the six children of a well-to-do miller, Golding Constable, who owned a watermill at Flatford, another at Dedham and two windmills at East Bergholt. These were the buildings and countryside which Constable said made him a painter. He went to schools at Lavenham and Dedham but he showed little academic ability, and decided when fairly young that he wanted to become a painter. His ambition was not matched by facility however, and his successful father made him work at milling when he was 18. His more sympathetic mother arranged a meeting with Sir George Beaumont, who encouraged him. At

19 he went to London and studied art in a haphazard fashion and it was not until he was 23 that he was admitted as a student to the Royal Academy. His progress was painfully slow in London and he only felt refreshed by his summer visits to his beloved Stour valley.

In 1804 Constable had a commission to paint an altarpiece *Christ Blessing Little Children* which you can see at Brantham Church (Tour 1). That shows clearly that such work was not his natural *métier*, although a later altarpiece at Nayland Church (Tour 1) shows his technical improvement five years later. His slow progress was partly because his ambition to paint 'true to nature' and not in the current fashionable style meant that he did not find favour at the conservative Royal Academy. He was also frustrated in love. When he was 35 he proposed to Maria Bicknell, granddaughter of the rich rector of Bergholt, who opposed the union. Their correspondence during the following five years is revealing, Constable moving from hope to despair and Maria patiently telling him: 'We have many painful trials in this life and we must learn to bear them with resignation'. But it was not until his father died and he inherited that Constable was able to marry his Maria.

Twelve happy years followed, during which Maria bore him seven children and when his delight in nature 'the brilliance of sunshine, the cooling freshness of morning dew, the fecundity of water-meadows, the drama of cloud-filled skies' were interpreted on canvas. The famous *Hay Wain* was exhibited at the Royal Academy in 1818 but received little praise in England. (Willy Lott's cottage at Flatford is the background of the *Hay Wain* and the nearby Manor House was the source of his *Valley Farm* painting). However, when it was shown at the Louvre in Paris Constable was lionized by the French and awarded a gold medal by the King of France. But his personal happiness was shortlived: his wife died in 1828 and Constable never recovered from her loss. He was made an RA in the year after her death, but as he wrote: 'The honour came too late now that I can no longer share it'. We are fortunate that we can share his vision and his works. It was not until French Impressionism reached England that his fellow countrymen realised the importance of his work, his ambition to record not only light but the movement of light and his use of patterns of colours to suggest forms rather than delineating them in detail. Some of his works may be seen at the Christchurch Mansion Museum in Ipswich (Tour 1) but most of his best work, over 300 paintings and sketches, are at the Victoria and Albert Museum, and at the National and Tate Galleries in London.

The Norwich School of Painters

The Norwich School of Painters were three generations of landscape artists working in the first half of the 19th century linked together by comradeship, an intriguing pattern of family and teacher-pupil relationships, and a devotion to subject matter taken from Norwich and the surrounding countryside. Their particular attraction for East Anglian visitors is that many of their works can be seen at the Norwich Castle Museum (Tours 5, 6 and 7) and that these, rewarding enough in themselves, also give the visitor an interesting insight into the local landscape of almost 200 years ago.

John Crome (1768-1821) was the father figure of the school. He was the founder of the Norwich Society of Artists in 1803, a society which lasted some 30 years and also produced artists of the stature of Cotman, Stannard, Stark and Vincent. John Crome was the son of a journeyman weaver and began life as an apprentice sign painter. Local patrons encouraged his obvious talent and he soon became a landscape painter and drawing master of merit. Like Constable, he painted the East Anglia countryside in a straight-forward truthful manner. No less than four of Crome's sons became painters, the most noteworthy being John Berney Crome.

John Sell Cotman (1782-1842) is the second best known of the school. The eldest son of a Norwich haberdasher, he lived and worked in Yarmouth and London a great deal of his life, returning to Norwich to become President of the Society of Artists in 1811. He was a supreme water-colourist, using a very modern style of abstract design, involving the portrayal of landscape with simplifed blocks of colour (see his *Greta Bridge* at the Norwich Castle Museum).

Robert Ladbrooke (1769-1842) was a printer's apprentice, but after his marriage to Crome's sister-in-law he also became a most competent landscape painter. He in turn taught Joseph Stannard (1797-1830) who became an accomplished painter in his tragically short life mainly, of Norfolk coastal scenes. His wife outlived him by 55 years and was a still-life painter. Joseph's brother Alfred Stannard (1806-1889) also painted but was mainly a drawing teacher. And one of his thirteen children, Eloise Stannard, not only excelled at still-life painting but connected the old Norwich School with the present century by living from 1829 to 1915.

You will enjoy seeing the work of painters from East Anglia, but will we ever know with certainty why the flat country of East Anglia, like that of Holland, has produced *so many* painters?

Places of Interest

The following pages contain information about things to see and places to visit in this part of Britain. You will come across many of them in the Tours. Such places have the number of the Tour printed after the county abbreviation, for example:
Fritton Lake, *Norf,* (Tour 6)
In most cases information is given only about places which can be visited, though occasionally a brief note has been added in order to satisfy the curiosity about an obvious landmark to which there may be no public access.

An asterisk* either before the place name itself or before the name of a building within the text means that the times of opening have been indicated in the list of page 124. The letters (NT) mean National Trust Property.

Aldeburgh, *Suff,* (Tour 2). Although but a small seaside resort, because of the music and arts festival held there each June, Aldeburgh has become perhaps the most widely-known town in Suffolk. The festival was started in 1948 by the late Benjamin Britten, who lived nearby, and concerts are held at the Jubilee Hall and in the local church, as well as at Orford, Framlingham, Blythburgh, and the new concert hall at Snape.

The town is on a narrow site beside the beach. Originally larger, much of the old town has suffered from encroachment by the sea. The most interesting building is the finely-restored 16th-century Moot Hall, a timber-framed and jettied construction with an outer stone staircase to the upper floor. George Crabbe, the poet, was born at Aldeburgh in 1755 and became curate of the mainly 15th-century parish church for a while.

Aldewood Forest, *Suff,* (Tour 2). One of the joys of driving from Ipswich, via Orford, to Aldeburgh – apart from the special pleasure of approaching the seaside – is in travelling through the pleasant forests of Rendlesham and Tunstall. These form two sections of a larger plantation called Aldewood Forest, the third being Dunwich Forest between Aldeburgh and Southwold. Aldewood amounts to some 14 square miles and was acquired by the Forestry Commission in the 1920's. Before afforestation it was heathland (bracken, heather and grass), some used for sheep grazing but none for agriculture, as it is poor soil for crops. The system of clearing the land and planting was similar to that at Thetford (see below), but unlike Thetford, a large number of Corsican and Scots pines were planted, together with the attractive Douglas fir. The economi-

23

cally mature trees are now being felled but there is no conversion depot and the timber is dealt with in the rides between each thinning block.

There are several picnic areas in these forests (two being indicated during Tour 2). They all have parking, and most have a waymarked walk or two starting from the picnic place. You will see red squirrels and fallow deer – and a few red deer if you are lucky. There is plenty of bird life; Dunwich Forest, running down almost to the seashore, is rich in sea and marsh varieties.

Anglesey Abbey

Anglesey Abbey, *Cambs,* (NT), is worth visiting to see both the contents of the house built on the site of the Abbey and the superb garden. An Augustinian priory was founded here in 1135 but largely demolished 400 years later. The old chapter house and vaulted canons' parlour remain, the chapter house being embellished now with mullioned and transomed windows. The property was bought by Lord Fairhaven in 1926 and in the 40 years until his death in 1966 he created a unique Georgian-style garden on this flat-looking site. And in the house he collected silver, jewellery, bronzes, Italian mosaics and paintings – the latter including Constable's *Waterloo Bridge*.

Attleborough, *Norf,* (Tour 7). St Mary's church has a 16th-century screen and rood loft stretching across both nave and aisles and reputed to be one of the finest in England. It is beautifully carved, with interesting wall paintings above the screen. The windows are also unusual – note particularly the four-petal flower pattern in the east window.

Audley End, *Essex,* lies one mile west of Saffron Walden. Although still an imposing house, it is but a fragment of the original great palace. The land was granted to Sir Thomas Audley, Henry VIII's Chancellor, nothing now remaining of the Benedictine monastery which was here before the Reformation. The original Audley End was built by Thomas Audley's grandson, the 1st Earl of Suffolk, in the first years of the 17th century. The earl became Lord High Treasurer to James 1 in 1614. James visited the place before it was finished and is supposed to have said: "It is to much for a king, but it might do well for a Lord Treasurer!"

The house had two courtyards, the principal one being 200 feet wide. Its plan was medieval and included a great hall with a screened passage. A hundred years after its completion the north, south and west sides of the great court were demolished under the direction of the dramatist and architect Sir John Vanbrugh. Later still the east range of the inner court was also taken down leaving the house as we now see it, together with its gardens designed by Capability Brown.

Entering the park through the 18th-century Lion Gate in Audley End Road we see the magnificent façade; all its windows mullioned and transomed, the biggest being the oriel in the centre which has 24 lights and illuminates the Great Hall. Elaborate patterns in stone enrich the porch arches, set between marble columns, and the doorways are beautiful examples of Jacobean carving. The south front has an arcade of nine bays divided by classical pilasters. The Great Hall is magnificent, the ceiling being supported by moulded tiebeams with carved hammerbeam brackets, and decorated with 40 plastered panels, each with a crest or badge. A marvellous oak screen fills one end of the hall, its three bays being divided by pairs of figures set on richly-carved pedestals. Flying cupids fill the spandrels of the archway in the central bay, above which are two smaller arches decorated with pierced arabesques. At the other end of the hall is a stone screen, with a stairway on each side, designed by Vanbrugh. The stairs lead to the long saloon, famous for its Jacobean ceiling, an elaborate work in plaster, depicting birds, ships and sea-monsters, divided by pendants. The restored dining room, drawing room and painted drawing room were designed by Robert Adam about 1762. The Braybrooke family lived at Audley End from 1762 to 1941 and the first Lord Braybrooke built the 'classical' buildings set at high points in the park, including the round temple, set on Ring Hill and the many-pillared Temple of Concord. Most of the 10 000 books in the great library were collected by his grandson, who was the first editor of Pepys. The stables escaped the great pulling down activity in the 18th century and therefore remain, with their gabled roofs and Tudor brickwork, as a humble reminder of the early magnificence of Audley End.

Aylsham, *Norf,* (Tour 5) on the river Bure, is a pleasant place, with many brick houses with Dutch gables. The manor was held by King Harold's brother and later by John of Gaunt, who is said to have founded the church in 1380. The latter is little altered since that time. Roses still grow on the graveyard of the landscape gardener Humphrey Repton, buried here in 1818, the epitaph (written by Repton himself) reading in part (referring to his ashes):

> *Mine shall give form and colour to the rose*
> *And while its vivid blossoms cheer mankind*
> *Its perfumed odours shall ascend to Heaven.*

*****Banham,** *Norf,* (Tour 7). The main attraction here is the zoo just south of the village. To the large collection of animals, and especially the collection of monkeys, has been added a separate show – a motor museum based on Lord Cranworth's collection of vintage cars.

Beccles, *Suff,* (Tour 4) lies on the Waveney river and is the southern limit of the Broads with its many holiday craft in the summer. Beccles was of course a flourishing port in earlier times – there is no lock between the town and the sea. It is an ancient town, but many of the Tudor buildings were destroyed by fire so the oldest are mainly Georgian. St Michael's church dominates the scene. Its massive detached bell-tower dates from the 14th century; 97 feet high, it houses a peal of ten bells. The south porch is unusual in being double-storied and decorated with elaborate niches, pinnacles and tabernacle work. The poet Crabbe was married here in 1783.

Blakeney, *Norf,* is a picturesque village with a bustling natural harbour, protected from the sea by Blakeney Point. This is an ideal place to take some exercise and enjoy the sea, dunes and salt marshes. There is a nature reserve at Blakeney Point where seabirds may be studied and seals may sometimes be seen. Blakeney's 13th-century church up on the hill has a fine hammerbeam roof and towers both at its west and east ends.

*****Blickling Hall,** *Norf,* (Tour 5) (NT) near Aylsham is a fine 17th century red-brick mansion. The Manor of Blickling belonged to the luckless King Harold. William the Conqueror bestowed it to the church so that it became the home of the bishops of East Anglia. Later the house was sold to Geoffrey Boleyn, whose family lived there until the execution of Anne by Henry VIII; it is now argued whether Anne was actually born at Blickling, but her parents certainly lived there, so it seems most probable. The present house was built by the Hobart family on the site of the earlier Hall; the architect is thought to have been the man who designed Hatfield House, as they have many similarities. The pictures and furnishings here are superb; the special features are the grand staircase and the long gallery, some 120 feet long, with an outstanding moulded plasterwork ceiling. The portraits include those of Elizabeth I and Sir Philip Sidney and, in the Peter the Great room, a tapestry of that Czar. The terraced grounds of Blickling Hall are also enchanting; there is an orangery, several avenues each of a particular species of tree, a beautiful lake and a mausoleum built in the shape of a pyramid.

Blythburgh, *Suff,* (Tour 4) is an intriguing little village standing on the edge of marshes. As in many Suffolk villages, the church now seems out of proportion with its surroundings. However, it is a splendid place dating from the 13th century and famous for the bench carvings of the Seven Deadly Sins. Its painted roof is interesting: the wings of the carved angels were shot off by Cromwell's troops but were later restored. (Nails on the nave pillars still show where the Cromwellians tethered their horses.)

Bocking, *Essex,* (Tour 3) is a village of many surprises with a factory which stands cheek-by-jowl with the 15th-century church. The Courtaulds were Huguenot refugees who fled to England in the 17th century; the factory originally made silk, but of course manufactures synthetics today. The village still maintains the timbered Woolpack Inn. Leaving the village you should not miss the post windmill, standing on rising ground. It is not in a good state now, but still impressive: it was built in 1690 and moved to Bocking in 1830. It is surprising that no one has made efforts to preserve it in better shape.

Boxford, *Suff,* (Tour 1) is an attractive little village with many timber-and-plaster decorated houses. Its church has an unusual timber porch. Note the odd mural tablet to 'Elizabeth Hyams, for the fourth time a widow who by a fall, that brought on a mortification was at last hastened to her end on the 4th May 1748 in her 113th year'.

Brancaster, *Norf,* is known best to golfers nowadays, but the Romans knew it as Branodunum, a naval base in its day. Two miles from the village is Brancaster Staithe, now National Trust property. Its coastguard station is the point for crossing to the island of Scolt Head, a Nature Conservancy-controlled island of some 1200 acres. The home of some thirty varieties of birds, it is of special interest to birdwatchers, being on a natural line of migration.

Brandon, *Suff,* (Tour 9). The most interesting thing about Brandon is that flint knapping still goes on here – a survival of the Neolithic mines at Grime's Graves, also seen during Tour 9. The custom is continued at the back of the Flintknappers Inn in Brandon.

Brantham, *Suff,* (Tour 1) has some unfortunate industrial buildings, but in the 14th-century church is an altarpiece, depicting Christ blessing children, painted by Constable in 1804 – a rare picture because Constable painted only one other religious subject, at Nayland.

*****Bressingham Gardens,** *Norf,* (Tour 7) with both informal gardens and steam engines should please the whole family. There are said to be over 5 000 different species of hardy perennials and Alpine plants growing in the parkland setting. The collection of steam engines is one of the largest in the country. There are three narrow-gauge railways in the grounds, one carrying passengers through two miles of the Waveney Valley.

Ormesby Broad

Broadland, *Norf,* (Tour 6). The Broads are shallow lakes in the valleys of the rivers Bure, Yare, Ant, Thurne and Waveney. There are some 46 of them, occupying some 2 000 acres of open water. The origin of the Broads remained a mystery for a long while until it was established beyond doubt that they were the flooded remains of medieval peat diggings. The peat was used as domestic fuel and also for heating sea-water to make salt; records suggest that this took place in the 13th and 14th centuries. (Aerial photography revealed that the diggings were in such geometrical lines that they could not have occurred naturally.)

Reed and sedge were harvested from Broadland areas for thatching for many years (the reed for the roofs, the sedge for ridging). The Bridewell Museum in Norwich has displays on this subject and the dioramas in the Norfolk Room of Norwich Castle Museum show the different animals and plants which exist in Broadland. Swallowtail butterflies are now confined to this area of East Anglia and can generally be seen in May, June and August. But naturalists have become concerned by the disappearance from the Broads of many water plants and animals during the last 30 years. It is thought that the use of fertilizers and other nutrients has caused the rapid growth of algae which prevent the natural growth of submerged water-weeds.

Bungay, *Suff,* (Tour 6) on the river Waveney is an ancient place and was an important river-crossing for the Romans. There was a castle of sorts here before the Normans arrived, later to be inherited by the Bigod family and a Bigod was made Earl of Suffolk by King Stephen. The *castle remains include a 12th-century twin-towered gatehouse and a ruined keep. Under the keep are the remains of what is thought to have been a mine-gallery, dug when the castle was under a ransom threat with the intention of firing the wooden supports and causing the keep to collapse.

The most obvious building in Bungay is the octagonal buttercross in the centre of the town, surmounted by a lead figure representing Justice; this was erected after an earlier market cross was destroyed by the fire which wiped out much of the town in 1688. Near the buttercross is a depiction of the Black Dog of Bungay who is supposed to have appeared in the local church in 1577 and 'wrought havoc'. The Black Dog is also known as Black Shuck or the Devil, who haunts the marshes to this day. St Mary's church was once the chapel of the 12th-century Benedictine nunnery; the upper part of its tower was built after the 1688 fire. Bungay is well known for printing and   29 leatherwork, and the printing works of Childs still keeps the blocks of Tenniel's drawings for *Alice in Wonderland,* which was produced here.

Bures, *Suff,* (Tour 1). There is a strong tradition that St Edmund was crowned king of the East Angles here in 855. The present St Stephen's Chapel is thought to be on the site of the wooden chapel where the coronation took place. If you follow the signpost to 'Chapel' you will find St Stephen's, dating from the 13th century and now with a thatched roof; it fell into disuse and was restored fifty years ago. It contains monuments of the de Vere family, brought from the vanished Colne Priory at Earls Colney in Essex. St Mary's church in the village also has a family monument to Sir William Waldegrave. Above the Waldegrave relic is a tablet to Mary Constable, aunt of the painter.

***Burgh Castle,** *Suff,* (Tour 6) is one of the best preserved of the Roman forts built from the Wash down the coast to Hampshire to resist Saxon raids. Known as Gariannonum, the castle housed a garrison of cavalry until the Roman withdrawal in the 5th century. The east wall was about 640 feet long, the north and south walls about 300 feet (there is no west wall – and whether there ever was is a matter of dispute). The walls are some 14 feet high although there was probably a parapet above that level originally. The east wall is all of 8 feet wide, resting on foundations of 11 feet, the north and south walls being marginally narrower. Formed of rubble concrete faced with square flints, the walls were not built in a continuous style but in sections, which were then bonded at the joins, and this can still be observed. The bastions, designed for use with *ballista* or catapults were added after the building of the original walls, it is thought. Roman coins and pottery have been found at Burgh Castle, as well as Saxon relics. It is believed that a Saxon King, converted to Christianity, gave the land inside the castle for the building of a monastery in the 7th century, and that this existed for some 200 years. When trying to imagine Burgh as a Roman fort is should be remembered that it guarded to some extent the nearby Roman port of Caister-on-Sea (see below). You have to walk across a field to reach Burgh Castle, but the ancient walls and the view over Breydon Water are worth it.

Bury St Edmunds, *Suff,* (Tour 11). 'A town famed for its pleasant situation and wholesome air' according to Defoe and 'a bright little town' according to Dickens, Bury St Edmunds remains a charming town with many Tudor and 18th-century houses and shops. It is essentially a town to wander about in, discovering all manner of interesting things – even the street names are intriguing: for example, Honey Hill, Hatter Street, and Skinner Street.

The slaughter of King Edmund and his canonization began the story of the town, although there was a small monastery at Bury founded in the 7th century by Sigebert, a descendant of the royal dynasty buried at Sutton Hoo, well before the death of Edmund in 870. The reason for Edmund's elevation seems to have been his great courage while being tortured by the conquering Danes and his refusal to renounce his Christian faith under the most terrible scourging. Thirty years later his beheaded body was brought to Bury, where hundreds of pilgrims then visited the shrine and miraculous events are said to have occurred. An abbey was built around the shrine in the 11th century. Little remains of that now – you may trace the outline of some of the walls in the Abbey Garden in the centre of the town: you may enter the garden through the enormous Abbey Gate, built in 1327 to replace the earlier edifice. An interesting plaque on the site of the high altar of the abbey church records that on 20th November 1214 the Barons of England swore at this place that they would obtain from King John a ratification of Magna Carta. (They did so the following year at Runnymede.)

Your steps will then lead you to the Abbot's Bridge, a structure of three arches dating from the 13th century and connecting the old monastery wall with that of the vineyard on the other side of the little River Lark (which runs into the Linnet). There are two churches nearby: St James', now being re-designed as a cathedral, and St Mary's. The latter has a superb nave, whose hammerbeams are carved to represent angels, and a chancel with a blue and gold wagon roof. The church also houses the tomb of Mary Tudor, sister of Henry VIII and Queen Dowager of France.

Carved Boss in St Mary's Church, Bury St Edmunds

Leaving the Abbey Garden, you are confronted by the delightfully-named Angel Hill. On one side stands the Athanaeum, a Palladian building of 1804. It is famed for the fact that Dickens gave readings in its great Assembly Hall (he stayed at the Angel Hotel almost next door). Not far away is Angel Corner (NT), the Queen Anne home of the *Frederick Gershom Parkington Collection of Clocks and Watches. One of the best of its kind in the world, the founder left the collection to the town in memory of his son, who was killed in the 1939-45 War. Other places to see (and it is best to wander about and stumble on them) are: the Theatre Royal in Westgate Street, a Regency theatre dating from 1819; Market Cross, designed by Robert Adam and now an art gallery; *Moyses Hall, a 12th-century house in Cornhill, now housing an East Anglian museum; and in Guildhall Street, the guildhall, partly dating from the 13th century.

Butley, *Suff,* (Tour 2) seems a remote village now, but there used to be a priory here covering no less than 20 acres. The old priory gateway, decorated with the coats of arms of East Anglian families, including that of Ranulf de Glanville, a crusader, is now a private house. You may pick out evidence of Norman architecture in the village church.

Caister Castle

*Caister Castle, *Norf,* (Tour 6). Although much of it is now a shell, the remaining west wall and slender tower above the wide moat give a good idea of the former beauty of this castle built by Sir John Fastolf in the 15th century in the style of a Rhenish Wasserburgh (the only example in England). Sir John had returned from fighting the French and was of course the knight on which Shakespeare based Falstaff. The real Sir John led the English archers at Agincourt, took part in the siege of Rouen and capture of Caen, became the Governor of the Bastille and helped negotiate peace with the French. He returned to Norfolk a rich man and built Caister to live in for the rest of his quiet life. On his death the castle passed to the Paston family – famous for their letter-writing – but the Duke of Norfolk challenged this inheritance and captured the castle with 3 000 men against a determined garrison of 28. Ironically, the Pastons re-possessed it on the Duke's death and retained it until the 17th century. An interesting feature of the castle is that it is built of brick – a comparatively new material for castle-building in the 15th century.

Caister-on-Sea, *Norf,* (Tour 6). There is not much to see of this once-important Roman port. In its day it stood on the north side of the huge sea inlet which ran into Broadland from the vicinity of Yarmouth. The port was built about AD 125 and was some 30 acres in area surrounded by a flint-faced wall ten feet thick. Some protection was available from the Roman soldiers stationed in the nearby Burgh Castle (see above).

Caistor St Edmunds, *Norf,* or Caistor-by-Norwich was the Roman town of Venta Icenorum. Established after the defeat of the Iceni about AD 70, not a lot of the cantonal town can be seen from the ground; however the whole pattern of streets on a grid-iron system, stretching far beyond the existing walls, may be seen from the air. Later the 50-acre site was added to with the building of forum, basilica and public baths. Then about AD 200 a strong defensive wall was erected around the centre of the town, making an inner secure area of some 35 acres. Some 20 feet high and 11 feet thick, this wall, some of which may be seen, was made of concrete faced with square flints and bricks. It was strengthened by towers and had a dry ditch 100 feet wide. The archaeological evidence suggest that the town was abandoned by the Saxons in the early 5th century. About 1300 the little parish church was built below the east wall of the Roman town, using much material from the ancient Roman walls. The church has a fine 14th-century font and an unusual wall-painting of St Christopher. The church is not open – you may collect the key from the address given in the porch.   33

Cambridge, *Cambs,* (Tour 12). Like so many other important towns, Cambridge owed its beginnings to its position – beside the river Cam where there was the best situation for a ford, later a bridge. This was also the highest point on the Cam navigable from the sea. The Romans established a camp on the little hill on the western bank of the river, not far from where Magdalene College is now, and the settlement which grew to cover some 25 acres, not being far from the meeting point of four Roman roads.

Later Cambridge developed as a trading centre, because goods could be carried by the Fen rivers and canals to and from the Midlands and the north of England more easily than taking them round the East Anglian seaboard. The town seems to have been deserted for periods after the withdrawal of the Romans, but the Danes wintered their army there in 875 and the Saxons have left a memorial by way of the tower of St Benet's church (appropriately enough near the present day Information Centre) – the oldest structure in Cambridge.

William the Conqueror entered the town in 1068 and built a castle on the west bank of the river. In the 12th century several monastic houses were founded in or near Cambridge, and some of these became colleges after the Reformation. The town grew in importance in the Middle Ages. Some time before 1200, a huge annual fair, the biggest in Europe, began to be held at which Continental goods, such as wine, could be bought and where country produce from East Anglia was sold; these fairs lasted five weeks. Booths were set out in rows according to the wares being sold, Garlick Row in the present town being a relic of that custom.

Oliver Cromwell attended Sidney Sussex College and became an MP for Cambridge in 1640. In the Civil War he made Cambridge the headquarters of the Eastern Counties Association and refortified the Norman castle, but little fighting took place in Cambridge. The town was not thickly populated originally – it was a place of houses and warehouses set among gardens and riverside wharfs. But after the draining of the Fens and the arrival of the railway Cambridge ceased to have a water-trading function and the university became the dominant factor in the town.

The University. 'Where is the university?' a stranger may ask in Cambridge. The answer is that the university is not one place but a collection of people. Each college is a separate self-governing body founded generally by wealthy patrons. The early colleges provided homes for groups of graduates pursuing their studies at the University. The Fellows are mainly responsible for running the colleges, and are supported by the college's income. In most cases the Fellows elect the Head of College, generally called the Master. Individual tuition is given by Fellows to undergraduates at the colleges, who also attend the lectures which are organized for all colleges at 'Old Schools' (opposite Great St Mary's church) and at other halls all over the city. The University's governing body consists of all office-holders in the Univeristy and colleges. The needs of Fellows are provided for in dining halls, libraries and chapels at each college, although many Fellows now live outside the colleges. There are some 9 000 undergraduates at Cambridge including 2 000 women.

Oddly enough, the exact beginnings of the university are not known. It is recorded that in 1209 there were disturbances in Oxford and that some students moved to Cambridge then – but it is thought that there must have been some rudimentary teaching going on at Cambridge before that date. A community of scholars was soon formed and, although they had no buildings of their own, they were recognized as an institution with their own Chancellor, masters and clerks (the latter were

Wren's Chapel,
Emmanuel College, Cambridge

the scholars). The first college to be established was Peter-
house in 1281, others following being Clare in 1326, Pembroke
in 1347, Trinity Hall in 1350, King's in 1441, Queen's in 1448,
Jesus in 1496, Christ's in 1505, St John's in 1511, Emmanuel in
1584, Girton in 1869.

Visiting the Colleges. You are welcome to visit most of the
colleges, to walk through all the courts and visit chapels and in
many cases the libraries and gardens. Notices outside colleges
lay down the minimum size of visiting parties.

Cambridge is one of the most beautiful cities in the world
and its architecture offers visitors weeks of study. However,
you may only be able to spend a day or two there, so we will
concentrate on a few of the many delights. It is only possible to
get around Cambridge on foot, so you must first park your car
in one of the many car parks near the city centre, or leave it a
little further away (parts of the centre of the town are pedestrianized).

The main streets fork into two at the Round Church in
Bridge Street in the north, the street nearest most of the big
colleges being called successively St John's Street, Trinity
Street, King's Parade and Trumpington Street, the other (with
more shops) Sidney Street, St Andrew's Street and Regent
Street.

Presumably you will wish to explore the colleges on your
own. However, if you would like a guided tour lasting some two
hours, you should go to the Tourist Information Centre in
Wheeler Street, where tours set out at 11 am and 2 pm daily
from May to October, and at varying times in the afternoon in
other months of the year.

*Christ's College in St Andrew's Street is a pleasant, smaller
college ideal as an introduction. It was built in the 1440's as a
college for teachers and then called God's House. Lady Margaret Beaufort, the mother of Henry VII, provided generously
for it in 1505 and there is a statue of her above the imposing
gateway facing the street. The charming first court is mainly
15th century, only the windows having been modernized in the
18th century. The Hall contains portraits of Field-Marshal
Smuts, Paley and Charles Darwin, all members or connected
with the college. But its most famous son was Milton and he is
commemorated in the mulberry tree in the famous gardens of
Christ's. It is still known as Milton's Mulberry Tree, and under
it he is supposed to have composed *Lycidas.*

*Jesus College is reached by walking down Sidney Street and
turning right into Jesus lane. The entrance, a paved walk
between red-brick walls is known as 'The Chimney'. The col-

lege was founded by Bishop Alcock of Ely, in 1497, following the suppression of a nunnery on the same site. You first come to the great gate tower, built by Alcock and thought to be on the site of the former nunnery gatehouse. It has three storeys, a spired ogee canopy, and above it a niche in which is a modern statue of Alcock. Notice the carving of a cock standing on a globe – this was a punning device on Alcock's name and will be found in wood or stone or on windows in the older parts of the college. The building left of the tower was originally built as a grammar school, that to the right was part of the nunnery; the west end of the chapel was converted into the Master's lodge. The first court is three-sided; the upper part of the building on the right houses the college library with furnishings of the 17th century. You next reach the cloister court – notice the fine roofs to the cloister walks, all part of the great builder Alcock's work. The arcades were rebuilt in the 18th century. In the northeast of the cloister court is an odd alcove which was once an entrance to the chapter house of the nunnery; this 13th-century doorway and windows are beautifully carved.

Next the intriguing chapel: although large it was the chancel of the nun's chapel. The first thing which will strike you is the great height of the building. It has gone through all sorts of changes over the years and Pugin restored it in the 1850's, but there is still much Early English stonework here. It is also a place to study the work of the 19th-century pre-Raphaelites – William Morris designed the decorated ceilings which were put in place in the 1860's. These have a strange look of tapestry although they are, in fact, of painted wood. Most of the stained glass in the ante-chapel was made by William Morris to the design of Burne-Jones; the colours are striking – hardly medieval – although they do not seem out of place.

The library of Jesus college has an autographed copy of the first edition of the first bible ever printed in America. It is in the Mohican tongue and printed in Cambridge Massachusetts – the connection with the college is that it was translated by a Jesus man who later became a missionary to the Indians. (Archbishop Cranmer, who was burnt for his Protestant beliefs, was a Jesus scholar, as was Samuel Taylor Coleridge.)

St John's College is reached by returning down Jesus Lane, turning right by the Round Church (of which more later) along Sidney Street to the junction with St John's Street; the college is opposite. St John's is a vast place, the only college to extend across the Cam (and you may get across comfortably in all weathers over the famous covered Bridge of Sighs). Like Christ's, St John's was founded by Lady Margaret Beaufort and stands on the site of the Hospital of St John founded before   37

1200. It has a magnificent gatehouse with brilliantly painted heraldic designs, the Beaufort arms flanked by fields of marguerites and Tudor roses. In an ornate canopy above is a statue of St John. Notice the fan-vaulting as you go through the gateway. The first court was built in 1520 and has hardly changed. The chapel, however, is comparatively new, designed by Sir Gilbert Scott in the 1860's; it contains some relics from the earlier chapel, including a recumbent figure of Hugh Assheton, also the stalls, which have a series of 16th-century misericords. The second court was built about 1600, a quiet place of brick with stone dressings. The third court was built in the 1620's and if you follow the central passage you find yourself not in a passage but in the enclosed Bridge of Sighs built in 1826. The New Buildings on the other side of the Cam are an interesting study of 19th-century Gothic.

You are now in the Cambridge Backs and it is pleasant to walk along the riverside, or to walk out into Queen's Road and return to Trinity college, next to St John's, from the gardens. *Trinity College* is the largest of Cambridge's colleges. It was founded by Henry VIII in 1546 but parts of it go back further, because it brought together nine older foundations. The Great Gate entrance is 16th century. Turning right through the gate you see the chapel; it contains the famous statue of Newton by Roubiliac, also others of Bacon, Macaulay and Tennyson. Trinity brought forth many great men – other sons were George Herbert, Marvell, Dryden, Byron, Housman and Vaughan Williams. The Clock Tower is at the west end of the chapel. The fountain in the centre of the Great Court is by Italian craftsmen and dates from 1602. The Hall has a fine hammerbeam roof and contains Holbein's portrait of Henry VIII, also paintings by Reynolds and Watts. Further on is Nevile's Court containing the lovely library designed by Sir Christopher Wren; it houses a wealth of statues and illuminated manuscripts. After Trinity College you should take a walk along the L-shaped Trinity Lane and visit Clare. *Clare College* is best seen from its beautiful garden on the far side of the equally lovely white-stone Clare Bridge. Founded in 1338 by Elizabeth de Clare, the original college building was destroyed by fire. The present charming court was built between 1638 and 1715, work being held up somewhat by the Civil War. It was partly designed by Robert Grumbold, son of the Thomas Grumbold who built the delightful Clare Bridge. Originally there were battlements at the top of the walls hiding the dormer windows: these were replaced in the 18th century by the much more attractive balustrade. The chapel is reached through a door in the northwest corner of the court. It was built in the 1760's and has an elegant octagonal ante-chapel famous for its glazed cupola. The altar painting of the Annunciation is by Cipriani. In the north window near the organ you may notice a depiction of Nicholas Ferrar, a member of Clare who founded a religious community at Little Gidding.

*King's College, Clare's neighbour is famous for its chapel, a poem in the Perpendicular style, and probably the most outstanding building in Cambridge. Its foundation stone was laid by Henry VI in 1446. The wonderful fan-vaulting of the roof was not completed until the 1500's. The stained glass is also unique, particularly as much other pre-Reformation glass has been destroyed. (The windows depict scenes from the Old Testament in the upper tiers, and from the New in the lower ones.) The chapel is certainly one of those places to sit and quietly absorb the atmosphere.

Work on the chapel was twice suspended firstly by the Wars of the Roses and then because of Henry IV's deposition. This resulted in two kinds of stone being used: Yorkshire limestone was the first and then, from nearer at hand, stone from Weldon in Northamptonshire. These different stones can be seen clearly, particularly on the north side of the chapel.

Although the chapel dominates the Great Court at King's, the Gibbs Building has a solid four-square attraction; it was designed in 1723 by James Gibbs. Most of the other ranges of buildings at King's are Victorian or of later date.

Other Cambridge Attractions

*The Fitzwilliam Museum, in Trumpington Street beyond King's College, contains a unique collection of Greek, Roman and Egyptian items, a collection of porcelain and pottery and wonderful oil paintings (including those by Constable, Cotman, Turner and Blake). Different rooms are exhibited at different times of day, so it is worth checking on these if you have a special interest.

The Botanic Garden in Trumpington Road beyond Trumpington Street is open (free) on weekdays. Part of the University Department of Botany, it is over a hundred years old and has a rock garden, scented garden and a chronological bed showing the dates when various plants were first discovered by explorers.

Great St Mary's Church almost opposite King's, is the university church and an attraction for young visitors or anyone who can climb the 123 tower steps for a superb view of the city.

The Round Church or the Church of the Holy Sepulchre, opposite St John's was built about 1130 on the plan of the Holy Sepulchre in Jerusalem. The round Norman nave remains, but the church was much restored in the 19th century. (Another of the five remaining round churches in England may be seen at Little Maplestead.)

*Castle Acre, *Norf,* (Tour 8). Castle Acre was one of the many manors in Norfolk granted by William the Conqueror to his son-in-law, William-de-Warrene. Entering the village you cannot miss the huge earthwork of the castle (one of the great ruins of England) up on the hill. The Normans built it of course, but some think that the earthwork may be as old as the Iron Age. Originally there was a central mound with a curtain wall and keep (nothing of the latter remains) surrounded by a 100-foot deep ditch. The chief remaining monument is the gateway, which now crosses the top of the village street. The huge outer bailey encircled the whole village. In the meadows by the river are the impressive ruins of the Cluniac Priory, built by William-de-Warrene's son and now looked after by the Department of the Environment. The gatehouse dates from 1500, the nearby prior's lodging is clearly Tudor. Passing through one then sees the impressive ruined priory, the west front of the priory church being ornamented with one of the most distinct examples of Norman blind arcading. The remaining foundations, now rising from the level lawns, can be traced as belonging to refectory cloisters, chapter house and kitchens. Castle Acre's parish church stands between the outer bailey and the priory precincts. Mainly 15th century, it has interesting poppy-heads and animals carved on the arm-rests of the benches and the Four Latin Doctors, Augustine, Gregory, Jerome and Ambrose are depicted on the wine-stem pulpit.

Castle Hedingham, *Essex,* (Tour 3) is a superb example of a solid, square Norman-Angevin type of keep castle. It belonged to the de Veres, Earls of Oxford, who, like many other powerful families, fought both for and against the King. The second Earl of Oxford fought against King John; the seventh represented the family at the Battle of Crecy. The ninth Earl married Edward III's grand-daughter and was a great favourite of King Richard II. A later descendant fought at Bosworth in 1485. The castle left the Oxford family in 1713.

The enormous stone keep was built in about 1140; it is 110 feet to the battlements with 20 foot-tall towers rising above them. The walls of the keep are 12 feet thick and it is thought that the mound on which it stands is natural. It will be seen that the entrance was not on the ground floor but on the first floor, in order to make a direct attack difficult. The northwest turret houses a spiral staircase which gives access to each of the floors whilst on the second floor there is a passage built into the wall which runs right round the top of the castle. The roof was originally surrounded by battlements. In 1919 the castle suffered a terrible fire – the effects can still be seen from the pink colouring on the inner walls.

Castle Hedingham's church has a red-brick tower of the 17th century, but there is an amazing lot of Norman work in the rest of the church, one of the unique features being three Norman doorways still with the original Norman doors (note particularly the great hinges). The nave walls are also Norman, as is the clerestory; the double hammerbeam roof is 300 years old, rich with carving of foliage and angels – the carved screen is also noteworthy.

Castle Rising, *Norf,* (Tour 8) was once an important port until the sea receded from it. The castle stood by the water in the 11th century: it is built on an ancient earthwork, for there was originally a Roman fort here. The remaining keep is one of the best-preserved Norman keeps in the country. The manor was originally given by William the Conqueror to his brother-in-law Odo but, after the latter rebelled he passed it on to his butler, William d'Albini, whose son built the castle. Later Queen Isabella, the 'She Wolf of France' was imprisoned here by her son Edward III for her suspected involvement in her husband's murder. The castle is now owned by the Howard family, although in the care of the Department of the Environment.

The Norman parish church of Castle Rising is worth visiting, to see particularly the decorated west front and inside a font decorated with frightening faces. Finally, Howard Bede house should be seen; founded by the Earl of Northampton in 1614 it provides homes for 'twelve poor women, single, 56 at least and no haunters of taverns'. If you happen to pass on a Sunday you will see today's twelve women attending church in their red cloaks and steeple hats just as their 17th-century predecessors did.

Cavendish, *Suff,* (Tour 11) is a pleasant village of pink-washed cottages about an attractive village green. Sir John Cavendish's old house is on the green; he was killed in 1381 by rebels because his son had treacherously killed their leader, Wat Tyler, after the King had given him amnesty.

Chelmsford, *Essex,* the county town owes its importance to its central position – its roads radiate to every part of Essex. Standing on a peninsula created by the rivers Chelmer and Can, it was originally a Roman settlement, Caesaromagus, thought to have been destroyed by Boudicca. The town did not start to attain importance again until about 1100, but still remained modest in size until the coming of the railway in 1843. During the last hundred years it has developed as an industrial centre, the most famous local company being Marconi. (The town was the first to adopt street lighting by electricity.)

The 15th-century parish church of Chelmsford became the cathedral of the newly-created see of Essex in 1914. Before that Essex came under the ecclesiastical rule of St Albans, and before that it was included in London's see. The splendid west tower is topped by pinnacled battlements and then a fine spire (of 1749) standing on an open lantern of pillars. The decorative flint and stonework of the south porch is especially noteworthy and very East Anglian in flavour: it was restored in the 1960's and the upper floor is now a library with a window commemorating the men of the American Air force who were stationed in Essex in the Second World War. There is much new work on the exterior, some of it representing the history of the town and the see – on the east corner of the south chancel St Peter is seen carrying a huge Yale key!

Inside, the church has been much altered over the years, more recently to accommodate the ceremonial needs of a cathedral. In the north chapel are memorials to the Mildmay family, once the local lords of the manor – Thomas Mildmay, a knight in Tudor times, is seen with his wife and fifteen children, described as 'fifteen pledges of their prosperous love'. And in the internal buttresses of the tower are a pair of rare banner lockers.

Chelmsford has a new county hall now and the old Shire Hall appears small in comparison – nevertheless it is a fine 18th-century building.

Chelsworth, *Suff,* (Tour 11) on the river Brett, has a 14th-century church worth a brief visit. It contains a fresco, described sometimes as a 'Doom' picture, above the chancel arch, which was discovered as late as 1849. It is thought to have been the work of a monk from Bury Abbey, to which the church belonged before 1538.

Chipping Ongar, *Essex,* is a small town with much historic interest. The name derives from the Old English 'chipping' meaning market and 'ongar' grazing land. It is thought that there was a Saxon settlement here and that part of the castle mound was built then. In 1154 it is recorded that the manor was owned by a famous Norman baron, Richard de Lucy, who built a moated castle on the mound; only a tree-covered mound

remains today. (Richard de Lucy was Chief Justice under
Henry II – he sided with the King against Becket, who excom-
municated him; weary of strife, he became a canon at Lesnes
Abbey (now on the outskirts of Woolwich in south London)
where he died.

The long High Street has several timber-framed buildings.
St Martin's church has Norman walls in the nave and chancel –
there are even traces of Roman tile around some of the church
windows. In the chancel wall is a little peephole facing the altar
and it is thought that the wall housed a tiny cell where an
anchorite lived. The great timber belfry is 15th century, a spire
being added 200 years ago. The 15th-century font is a curiosity,
carved as an octagon from a square block, leaving odd 'towers'
at the corners. Near the altar you will see a black marble
memorial to Jane Pallavicini, a daughter of Sir Oliver Cromwell (not the Lord Protector but a relative).

Ongar's Congregational chapel is also of interest because of
two of its famous sons, David Livingstone the explorer (he
trained here for the church) and the pastor Isaac Taylor. The
latter was a prolific writer and his two daughters, Ann and
Jane, wrote many books and hymns (see Lavenham).

Clare, *Suff,* (Tour 11) is an interesting old town on the bank of
the Stour where you may see pargetting (the application of
moulded plaster) decorating many cottages – note particularly
the Ancient House near the church. The lordship of the place
was given by William the Conqueror to the FitzGilberts, who
later adopted the name de Clare. Only fragments of the castle
remain. In 1866, when part of the bailey of the castle was being
excavated to make way for the railway station, a reli-
quary cross of gold and pearls was found. In a small cavity were
fragments of wood thought to be relics of the True Cross. It was
presented to Queen Victoria – ironically enough it is thought
now that it may have belonged to her ancestor Edward III
whose grand-daughter lived at Clare Castle; she was married
three times but was a widow at 28.

The huge parish church in the centre of the town has a
13th-century tower, containing unique Tudor heraldic glass in
the east window and a fine old brass lectern. Across the river is
Clare Priory, found in 1248 as an Augustinian monastery.
Banished at the Reformation, the Augustinians returned to
Clare in 1953. The building they now use was a 17th-century
house built among the ruins of the former Prior's House and
Cellarer's Hall. The grounds are encircled by the River Stour,
(which was diverted by the monks) and are a pleasant place to
walk in.

Coggeshall, *Essex,* (Tour 3) on the river Blackwater was important as a medieval wool centre. *Paycocke's House, (NT) is a finely decorated Tudor wool-merchant's house, beautifully panelled inside. Their family brasses can be seen in the 15th-century church nearby. What is left of a Cistercian abbey may be discovered near the river; these remains are incorporated into a farmhouse and are said to be an example of the earliest medieval brick building in England.

Across Long Bridge are the ruins of Little Coggeshall Abbey, founded by Stephen in 1140. You can still see the gate-chapel and the abbot's lodging, (now connected by a corridor to a house of a 16th-century Paycocke), and a small guest-house dating from the 12th century. The latter is of interest because its very small bricks are the earliest known since Roman times; it is thought that they were made at Tilkey on the outskirts of Coggeshall.

Colchester, *Essex,* has been described as a town standing at the junction of British history with prehistory. Here King Cunobelin (Shakespeare's Cymbeline) became king of southeast Britain and built his capital called *Camulodunum,* after Camulos, God of War, in about 10 AD. It was on a slope above the river Colne to the southwest of the modern Colchester. Its outer dykes are still visible in the Lexden Park area. The Roman army under Emperor Claudius destroyed the town during the conquest in AD 43 (when Cunobelin's son Caractacus was taken as prisoner to Rome) and built a new one on the present site. Seventeen years later Boudicca and her Iceni revolted against the Romans and sacked Colchester. The revolt was shortlived and the Romans set about building an even stronger Colchester early in the second century. Enclosing a town of some 100 acres, the walls were nine feet thick and some 18 feet high: what remains of these can be seen mostly on the west side of the town, where the huge Balkerne Gate survives in all its Roman glory. And the principal streets of Colchester still follow those of the Roman town. After the departure of the Romans the town declined rather (except for its famous oyster trade) but the Normans felt it important enough to build a castle here, with the largest keep in England.

And the castle is a good place to start a visit to Colchester. The Normans built it over the surviving foundations of the Roman temple to Claudius – these can still be seen and, almost unbelievably, the marks on the stone caused by the great fire during the sacking by Boudicca also remain. Although of Norman architecture, the castle incorporates much Roman material. It resembles the White Tower of London in several respects and is thought to have been designed by the same man. Apart from an attack by the French against King John in the 13th century, the castle saw little action until the Civil War, when Colchester was held for King Charles and withstood a siege of three months. The Cromwellians then captured it and put the Royalist leaders Sir Charles Lucas and Sir George Lisle on trial, during which they were held in the castle and then executed by a firing squad.

In the late 17th century a local ironmonger was given permission to demolish the castle. Luckily for us the task was beyond him and he only succeeded in removing the top storey.

The castle now houses Colchester's* museum, which is particularly rich in pre-historic items; it also has an outstanding display of Roman relics of all kinds.

Going down Long Wyre Street from the castle you will reach St Botolph's Priory, just outside the Roman wall. It is a ruin but a very impressive one. The priory was founded in the 11th century and became Augustinian in about 1100, the first house of that order in England. The remaining west front shows rich arcading; inside, the nave has seven remaining bays with pillars of some six feet in diameter. The church suffered much during the Cromwellian bombardment.

St Botolph's Priory, Colchester

Returning along Vineyard Street and Trinity Street, you can see Holy Trinity church. Its Saxon tower, close to the street, contains much Roman brickwork – look at the jambs and the head of the doorway to the tower. Inside there are some 14th-century and 15th-century items – and much 19th-century restoration.

Crossing the High Street and going up West Stockwell Street you come to the Dutch Quarter. Here are many timbered houses once occupied by Flemish weavers, who came over originally as refugees.

The Lexden Dykes may be seen some three miles outside the town on the A12 near Beacon End. A footpath follows the most westerly dyke for about a mile; the dykes were originally built to defend the land between the Colne in the north and the Roman river in the south.

Colchester Zoo is two miles out of the town on the B1022, at Stanway Green.

Cottenham, *Cambs,* (Tour 12) is a large village set in the middle of orchards. The diarist Samuel Pepys knew this place well, for no less than 26 Pepys families once lived here. One of them, Katherine Pepys, paid for the restoration of the church tower, which fell in 1617. Now a strange hybrid, its lower parts are 15th century with bulbous 17th-century pinnacles crowning stepped battlements. The church has several interesting things inside, including 19th-century benches with carved ends.

Cromer, *Norf,* (Tour 5). 'Discovered' by the Victorians, the old fishing village of Cromer was turned into a watering place, complete with the grandest of hotels which still lord it over the sea front, while the remaining ancient cottages keep respectfully in their place, behind. The church on the top of the cliffs has a tower of 160 feet (one of the highest in Norfolk) which served as a lighthouse before the building of the existing one (which incidentally may be visited). Cromer's hero is the late Henry Blogg, coxswain of the Cromer lifeboat until his death in 1954; there are memorials to him both inside and outside the town church. He was known as the most decorated lifeboatman in Britain, winning both the George Cross and the British Empire Medal as well as the RNLI's Gold Medal no less than three times. Stories of his bravery may be heard in Cromer pubs; most of his heroic rescues were from the nearby Haisboro' sands.

Cromer crabs are reputedly the best in England and it is well-worth watching the Cromer fishermen at work in their
strange little crab boats. Children may enjoy *Cromer Zoo,

which covers five acres; it is proud of its breeding record, having even bred lion cubs twice.

Diss, *Norf,* (Tour 7) is a fine old market town built around a six-acre lake called The Mere. The High Street offers an interesting variety of Tudor, Georgian and Victorian architecture and a stroll will reveal in the side streets several timber-framed houses with carved corner-posts; one, in St Nicholas Street, shows a scene of the Annunciation. St Mary's church is 14th century and has two chancel chapels built by local trade guilds. The church is proud of its 15th-century rector, John Skelton, Poet Laureate to King Edward and tutor to Henry VIII.

Doddington, *Cambs,* (Tour 10) is mainly of interest for its 13th-century church. Its windows contain glass designed by William Morris and Rosetti and it has an unusual wood carving depicting Christ and the woman of Samaria. The rector here in Tudor times, Christopher Tye, was a considerable composer, the most well known of his compositions being the carol *While Shepherds Watch their Flocks by Night.*

Earls Colne, *Essex,* (Tour 3) is the largest of the Colne group of villages. Its attractive High Street has timbered houses as well as 18th-century ones. St Andrew's church has a splendid battlemented tower of the 16th century but is of little interest otherwise. Leaving the village towards Colchester you may see the chimneys of Colne Priory, an 18th-century Gothic house in brick on the site of a medieval priory. The monuments to the de Vere family removed from that priory may be seen at nearby St Stephens church at Bures (see Bures).

East Barsham, *Norf,* (Tour 8). The village is renowned for its Tudor manor house. Both the house and the huge gatehouse have superb carved and moulded brickwork. The gatehouse has graceful turrets and calls to mind an upturned footstool. Sir Henry Fermor built the manor in the 1520's. It was badly neglected but carefully restored in the 1920's. The interior may only be seen by special appointment between July and September.

East Bergholt, *Suff,* (Tour 1). Such is his fame it is almost superfluous to say that East Bergholt was the birthplace of East Anglia's most famous artist, John Constable, in 1776 (see p20). Naturally, the village attracts many sightseers in the summertime and it is best to get there early in the day to avoid traffic jams. St Mary's church is unusual in that it has an unfinished   47 tower: the local legend is that as builders tried to construct the tower by day the Devil came nightly and destroyed the work. Whatever the truth, the church's bells are housed in a 16th-century timber bell-house close to the church; the bells hang upside down and are rung by hand. The church contains a memorial to Constable's wife Maria (whose grandfather was a rector here). The artist's parents are buried in the churchyard. (See also Flatford Mill.)

East Raynham, *Norf,* (Tour 8). This village is famous for the owner of Raynham Hall, which you will see from the road (it is not open to the public) – the Second Viscount Charles Townshend. Commonly known as 'Turnip Townshend', he introduced the turnip to England. It was a 'cleaning crop' and its use led the way to the 'Norfolk Four-Course Rotation' system which was later in common use throughout the land.

Ely, *Cambs,* (Tour 10). From whatever direction you approach Ely you will be granted a superb view of the huge dominating cathedral. It is not difficult to visualize Ely as the island in the Fens it once was until the draining of the Fens in the 17th and 18th centuries. The story of Ely goes back to Britain's Dark Ages and the birth of Etheldreda, one of the daughters of the East Anglian King Anna in the 7th century. She was married to a prince who was lord of a Celtic tribe which lived in the Fens. But Etheldreda became a nun and founded a monastery at Ely in AD 673. After her death her burial place at Ely became a shrine; she was canonized, the shrine attracted many pilgrims, and many miracles were supposed to have happened. (Etheldreda's name was shortened to St Audrey and the fairs at which trinkets were sold in her name gave rise to the word 'tawdry'.)

At the time of the Norman Conquest Ely was the refuge of Hereward the Wake and many dispossessed Anglo-Saxons. According to legend, the Abbot of the abbey then established at Ely made a secret pact with William and led the Normans to the island while Hereward was absent.

The Cathedral. The building of the cathedral began in 1083 under a Norman Abbot, Simeon, and took 268 years to complete. The north and south transepts (which still survive) were built first, then a central tower (which later collapsed), then the choir. And then St Etheldreda's remains were brought to the cathedral to be buried with those of her sister and a niece who had followed her as Abbess. Henry I then supported the creation of a bishopric of Ely (thus saving it from destruction at the time of the Dissolution of the Monasteries, because cathedrals were not of course dissolved). The beautiful Lady Chapel was

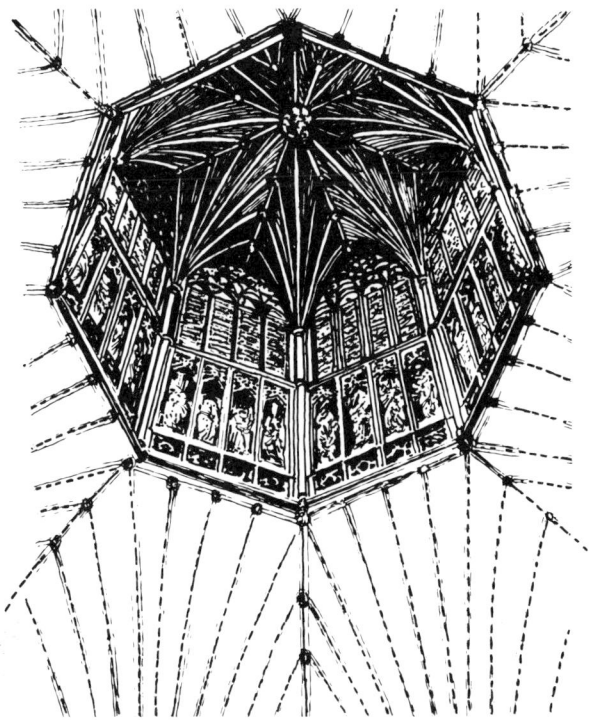

Lantern of the Octagonal Tower, Ely Cathedral

added in the 14th century – a poem to English Gothic. But soon after, the great central tower built by the Normans crashed down, destroying part of the choir. Happily, the Sacristan of the time, Alan of Walsingham, was something of an architectural genius: he designed an octagonal tower to replace the square one, crowning it with the superb wooden lantern. The work took 26 years, a comparatively short time considering all the fan-vaulting and delicate tracery work. It is reckoned that the tower supports a weight of no less than 400 tons of wood and lead.

Entering the cathedral through the Galilee Porch you are immediately struck by its great length – 537 feet – and its beauty is enhanced by the fact that there is no longer a stone screen breaking one's clear view of the nave's Norman arches, which are surmounted by triforia of double arches and high clerestories. On the right-hand side of the nave you may notice Ovin's Cross: this refers to Owen, St Etheldreda's steward, thought to have been a Celt. Bede tells of how, when dismissed   49 the service of Etheldreda, he became a monk and was later canonized. Passing underneath the octagon you will see the scenes from the life of Etheldreda, carved on the corbels of the eight shafts of the structure in the 14th century. The choir stalls are of the same period and contain no less than 54 miserere seats carved with amusing figures. The transepts and chapels contain most elaborate carvings, note particularly the highly decorated roofs, some with angels as hammer bearers.

The separated Lady Chapel should be visited; the windows are plain now and the light and the chalk stone of the building gives an extraordinary sense of white lightness. The roof here spans 46 feet and is said to be the widest vaulted roof in England. Finally, if you have the energy you may climb the 215 feet of the West Tower to be rewarded with a marvellous view of the Wash and, if it is a clear day, of Cambridge.

Epping Forest, *Essex,* over 5 000 acres of woodland, is the largest surviving part of the huge Forest of Essex. It stretches from the town of Epping to the borders of built-up London at Chingford. It is traversed by the busy A11 but nevertheless provides many quiet walks. The woodland is of oak and silver birch and, most typically, of hornbeam – the latter have been cut for centuries when commoners had the right to do so; such lopping has resulted in trees of fantastic shapes.

The Forest of Essex was made subject to the Norman forest law, which imposed harsh penalties on any poaching of deer. It was then royal property and mainly used for hunting. By the 19th century large areas were being enclosed and there was a likelihood of the forest being swallowed up altogether – fortunately the Epping Forest Act of 1871 transferred ownership to the Corporation of London 'for the enjoyment of the people'. (This was a pioneering act which led to others which protected commons on the borders of other parts of London.) There are fallow deer in the forest still.

High Beech is considered one of the most attractive parts of the forest. Amresbury Banks, 1½ miles south of Epping church on the A11 is an Iron Age fort – the rectangular bank and ditch can still be discerned beneath a covering of trees. Despite the lack of historical evidence, tradition still insists that Amresbury Banks was the scene of Boudicca's last battle. A final curiosity: outside the park of Copped Hall, 1½ miles south of the town of Epping, is Wood House, built in imitation of the Ancient House in Ipswich.

Euston, *Suff,* (Tour 9). The village is interesting in that it was moved to its present site in the 17th century because it got in the way of the view from the Duke of Grafton's Euston Hall. The church now stands in splendid isolation in the park. Dedicated, unusually, to St Genevieve, it was re-built in 1676 in the Classical style; the fine wood-carving of the pulpit, reredos and screen are attributed to Grinling Gibbons.

The trees in the park were originally planted under the direction of the diarist John Evelyn, the park itself being designed by William Kent. The tree-planting was later criticized by Horace Walpole who said it made the lawn 'look like the ten of spades'.

Fakenham, *Norf,* (Tour 8) is a pleasant market town on the river Wensum with Georgian houses in the market square. Its church is partly 14th century, but was much restored in the 19th when the angel hammerbeam roof was built over the nave. The sedilia and piscina are late 14th century.

Felbrigg, *Norf,* (Tour 5). *Felbrigg Hall (NT) is assoiacted with two families, the Felbriggs and the Wymondhams. The Hall, with its Jacobean front of brick and stone dressings was built about 1620, with later additions. The words *Gloria Deo in Excelsis* are picked out in tracery on the parapet of the south front. Inside, the Cabinet Room was designed by James Paine in 1750 to display the pictures bought by the second William Wymondham on his tour of Europe. Other parts of the house have excellent examples of stucco plastering. The pleasant grounds were laid out by Humphrey Repton in the early 19th century and there are an orangery and an unusual octagonal dovecot. Felbrigg's church is also in the hall grounds and is worth discovering: it contains outstanding brasses and other memorials to the Wymondham family, one executed by Grinling Gibbons and another by Nollekens.

Felixstowe, *Suff,* is another of Suffolk's seaside places which developed from a village when the railway reached it in 1877. It is not a quiet spot, but a pleasant enough place for children to paddle or swim (the beach is of shingle with some sand at low tide). With an aqualung you may see the underwater remains of the Roman Fort of Walton Castle, some hundred yards from the shore. A walk may be taken south of Felixstowe to see the artificial harbour on the coast looking across the Orwell estuary towards Harwich. Walking north you will reach Felixstowe Ferry and be able to gaze across the river Deben where it reaches the sea.

Fenland, *Cambs,* (Tour 10). The Fens lie in a huge area between King's Lynn and Sleaford in the north and roughly between Ely and Ramsey in the south. Four Fenland rivers run through it, the Wissey, Wellan, Nene and Great Ouse, all emerging eventually into the Wash. These waters fight a battle with the tidal waters which force their way up the rivers from the sea, often causing floods. The Romans dug dykes to hold the sea back and also built causeways to enable them to cross this watery area. All this work ceased when they departed and it was not taken up again until the Normans arrived and established their religious houses at Ely and Thorney. A famous churchman, Bishop Morton, supervised the cutting of the channel which still bears his name.

But it was not until the 17th century, after the Dissolution of the Monasteries and the great capitalistic drive which followed the event, that the Fens were tackled seriously. The great Dutch engineer, Cornelius Vermuyden, was brought over to supervise much of the work. Then the rivers were straightened, or canalized, and huge artifical drains were dug, including the Forty Foot (or Vermuyden's Drain), the Sixteen Foot, the Old Bedford and the Middle Level Main Drain. These man-made rivers were given high banks because they often flow well above the surrounding countryside, the water being pumped up into them (much of the Fens are below sea level). The Fens must have been an amazing sight when they had hundreds of windmills pumping the water up into the canals; later they were superseded by steam power (the coal coming up the waterways) and later still by diesel engines. One pumping windmill survives at Wicken Fen.

The Fens consist of rich peat and grow super cereal and other crops. But as they are drained and the peat dries the land is sinking lower and lower. Fenmen are a tough lot though. One of their skills is in ice skating; when the water freezes they travel great distances on skates. A legend says that King Canute used to skate to Ely, and it as likely a tale as the others told of him.

North of Southery is an area called the Marshlands. Unlike the Fens, this land is above sea level and does not consist of peat but a silty loam. Another peculiarity hereabouts are the Washes, or Washlands, in Fenland. These areas of low-lying land are deliberately not inhabited and are reserved for summer grazing; if winter floods threaten, the sluices are opened to flood these empty pastures to avoid flooding elsewhere.

Finchingfield, *Essex,* owes much of its charm to the picturesque setting of its tiled and thatched cottages grouped around a green, which slopes down to the river Pant. The church dominates the rising ground; its Norman tower is surmounted by an 18th-century wooden lantern. The 14th-century south porch has double doors of that period decorated with traceried panels and carvings of the Crucifixion, birds and other figures. Inside, the architecture dates from the 13th to the 15th centuries – notice the fine chancel screen. The many memorials include those to William Kempe who lived at Spain's Hall in the 17th century and to the Ruggles-Brises, more recent residents there.

Spain's Hall is a beautiful Tudor building with mullioned windows and a porch rising the full height of the house. It is set in extensive grounds, decorated with a lake created from two mill-ponds.

Finchingfield

Flatford Mill, *Suff,* (Tour 1) on the river Stour is reached down a narrow lane from East Bergholt – a very crowded lane because so many people want to see Willy Lott's cottage, the background for the famous *Hay Wain,* and the manor house featured in *The Valley Farm.* However, there is an adequate parking place and anyone familiar with Constable's paintings will enjoy seeing the scenes he painted with their own eyes. The mill-house, cottage and manor house now belong to the National Trust and are rented to the Council for the Promotion of Field Studies who run a wide range of residential courses there.

Framlingham, *Suff,* (Tour 2) standing on a little hill, is a charming town which was once an important centre. The main feature of the famous *castle is the great curtain wall and its 13 towers. It was in fact one of the first castles in England built as a curtain wall without a predominant keep (as at Orford, see below). The notion of such a fortress came from the castles of the Saracens and was imitated by the returning Crusaders. (An unusual feature of the castle is that each of the 13 towers had 53 direct access to the inner courtyard.) There was originally an inner bailey and an outer one enveloping what is now the town of Framlingham – a truly great fortification. The curtain wall is some 44 feet high; the towers were built between 1177 and 1215. There is no local stone, so it had to be brought by sea and up the Ore river all the way from Barnack in Northamptonshire. The wall walk, with its superb views across the countryside, is reached by a spiral staircase in one of the towers. The soaring Tudor chimneys were added later of course – all but two of them are decorative.

The castle has an involved history: its first owner was Roger Bigod whose son Hugh was made Earl of Norfolk. He rebelled against Henry II and the castle was captured by the King. His son rebelled against King John, who also took the place. A later owner was Lord Thomas Mowbray, a favourite of Richard II who made him Earl Marshal of England and Duke of Norfolk (which title still survives). By the 15th century the Howard family inherited the castle and that title. In 1553 Mary Tudor made Framlingham her base from which with an army of 13 000 men she attacked the supporters of Lady Jane Grey and it was here that she was proclaimed Queen of England. Eventually the old buildings inside the curtain walls were destroyed and a poorhouse built there; this is now partly used as a courthouse.

Framlingham's church, with a 15th-century tower and beautiful fan-vaulting, has a huge range of Howard family monuments, including the helmet of the First Duke of Norfolk worn during his defeat of the Scots at Flodden. It may be noticed that the effigy of Henry Howard, Earl of Surrey, has the coronet lying beside its head: that was to signify that he was in fact beheaded. (A later Howard married into the Arundel family bringing Arundel castle in Sussex into the Norfolk family, who still live at Arundel.)

Fritton Lake, *Norf,* (Tour 6). Though a commercial venture, it is an attractive spot: the lake is over two miles long and edged with pleasant gardens. Boats may be hired and there is also fishing, an adventure playground and a putting green – a good place for children.

Glandford, *Norf,* is a model village of flint and brick houses built by Sir Alfred Jodrell of nearby Bayfield Hall. The famous Shell Museum contains shells (first collected by Sir Alfred, who was a great traveller), pottery, jewellery and relics of Pompeii. The church of St Martin was rebuilt by the knight in memory of his mother.

Godmanchester, *Cambs,* (Tour 12) was an important Roman settlement on the crossroads of Via Devena (from Colchester to Chester) and Ermine Street (which linked London and York). It is a pleasant town with many 16th- and 17th-century timbered houses. The lovely carved choir stalls in the 14th-century church are said to have been brought here from Ramsey Abbey after the Dissolution of the Monasteries. The Elizabethan grammar school is near the causeway and bridge across the Ouse which leads to Huntingdon.

Gosfield, *Essex,* (Tour 3). Gosfield Hall is basically a Tudor building, though much restored. The red-brick west front preserves its original appearance, having diaper patterns in blue. Now owned by the Mutual Households Association and a house for retired people, it is also open to the public. The wife of one of the owners, John Knight, erected a great monument to him in the local church on his death in 1733. She later married Earl Nugent and then had the monument screened so that she would not see it when she went to the church!

Grantchester, *Cambs,* (Tour 12). What would Rupert Brooke, the Golden Boy poet who died in the First World War think if he knew that everyone remembers Granchester because of his nostalgic poem of that name, with the memorable lines:

> *And stands the church clock at ten to three*
> *And is there honey still for tea?*

Brooke came to live here with the Stevenson family at The Orchard in 1909 and wrote the lines, full of homesickness, in Berlin. He later lived with the Ward family at the Vicarage, a red-brick 17th-century house. Tennyson and Byron were also fond of this village. The church of St Andrew and St Mary is 14th and 15th century and has a beautiful chancel in the Decorated style. If the weather is kind this is a good place for a stroll along the River Cam.

Great Yarmouth, *Norf,* (Tours 2 and 4). This big seaside town, with a population of some 50 000, is almost an island: the rivers Bure and Yare flow into the wide Breydon Water to the west of the town, the Yare flowing out of the Breydon and almost reaching the sea, but then turning south and running for three miles parallel to the coast before turning west and flowing into the sea. Most of Great Yarmouth lies on this spit of land with the sea on one side and the Yare on the other. There is a sandy beach and the water is shallow. Though it is a noisy resort, it has some interesting sights.

Yarmouth became 'Great' when it received its charter from Henry III in 1272. From the 11th to the 17th century the town was invaded annually by fishermen from the Cinque ports who made the 'herring voyage', the herring fair for the sale of salt herrings being controlled by the Barons of Hastings. It has been a perpetual concern of Yarmouth to keep the harbour mouth open and free from silt; in the 16th century it is recorded that the church plate and bells were sold to pay for work on the harbour. The fishermen also suffered a great deal during the time when the Dutch navy was powerful and Dutch fishermen used to poach the local waters. The herring industry flourished in the early years of this century: some thousand vessels, many of them from Scotland, were recorded in 1913 and in those days Scots fisher-women arrived as well to help with the herring gutting ashore. The trade has died in recent years, but Yarmouth now has a flourishing entrepôt trade – you will see ships from the Baltic, the north of England and London on the quays. It is also concerned with the North Sea Oil industry.

The older part of the town (South Denes Road and Southgates Road) was built facing not the sea but the River Yare. The sea front was developed later. Then an extraordinary number of narrow alleys were built (because of the pressure on land) between the two, so that there were no less than 145 Rows (as they were called). Originally named, they were later, like New York streets, known by numbers and you can see typical merchants' houses in Rows 117 and 111 which have been restored by the Department of the Environment; some of the rooms are panelled and have fine plaster ceilings. Most of the old Rows were destroyed in the Second World War.

The Market Place is a busy part of the central town. Nearby you may see the Fishermen's Hospital, almshouses ranged round a courtyard. Next to the hospital is Sewell House, where Anna Sewell, author of *Black Beauty* was born in 1820. St Nicholas church has a reputation of being the largest parish church in England with a floor area of 23 000 square feet. Parts of the structure are 12th–13th century, but the interior was completely burnt out in an air-raid in 1942, so you mainly see restored Gothic; much of the furniture has been brought in, for example, the beautiful Georgian pulpit comes from another Yarmouth church. Walking westwards from the church, you will come to the River Yare and the quays. On your right is the northwest tower, the best-preserved of such towers along the old town wall. Moving south past many fine merchants' houses dating from the 16th century you arrive at *No 4 South Quay; the Elizabethan House, (NT); it was built in 1596 but has been furnished as a merchant's house of the 17th century. An intriguing legend is that in 1648 when the Cromwellian bailiff of the town lived here, a meeting was held at this house at which the execution of Charles I was agreed.

Further south again, you find the Customs House, built in the 17th century with a 19th-century porch. Not far away in Tolhouse Street is the Tolhouse Museum. Built in the 14th century and one of the oldest municipal houses in England, it now houses a museum of local history. Youngsters will want to see the dungeon, once the town's prison.

Various sea and river trips can be taken from Great Yarmouth of course – one to the Scobie Sands may give you the chance of seeing seals.

Greensted, *Essex,* is a great place for pilgrimages for it has the oldest wooden Saxon church in the country. But whether this was also the church where the martyr King Edmund's body was rested for a night on its journey from London to Bury St Edmunds, to be placed in a newly-built shrine, cannot be proved. The history relates that the body was rested in a *lignea capella*, which (meaning wooden church) would certainly conform with a description of the wooden church at Greensted. In any case it has been scientifically proved that the wooden walls of Greensted are dated well before the reburial of Edmund in 1013, because the wood is dated to about 850. The way in which the Saxons used the oak trunks is plain to see. Each one was split in three, the two outer beams being used to build the wooden walls, the central planks for roof and sills. The uprights were fixed into grooved beams running along each side of the nave. The horizontal supporting beams were found to be rotting during a restoration in 1848, so they were cut and now rest on a supporting brick plinth (built to restore the walls to their original height). The roof was formerly thatched and the church lit from windows in the west wall and chancel.

Other alterations have been made over the centuries. The Normans built a chancel of flint and this was rebuilt in brick about 1500. In the 16th century the roof was tiled and the domestic-looking leaded dormer windows added; a tower and belfry were also built on at this time. The church has a small painted panel – thought to be what remains of a 15th-century screen – depicting the martyrdom of King Edmund. Another odd link with Edmund are the wooden covers of a bible and prayer book made from the timbers of the tree under which he is supposed to have been martyred. The tree, at Hoxne, fell a hundred years ago – almost unbelievably a Danish arrowhead was found embedded in the trunk (this is not a myth as the arrowhead may be seen still).

57

***Grimes Graves,** *Norf,* (Tour 9) is a fascinting place to visit. The significance of these Neolithic flint mines is discussed on page 13 of the Introduction. On the 40 acre site, now looked after by the Department of the Environment, are the remains of some 400 mines. Many of them can only be identified by depressions in the ground, but one mine has been kept open so that visitors may descend some 30 feet to gain some idea of the accomplishment of the primitive miners of 4 000 years ago. They dug the flint out with sharpened deer antlers, hundreds of which have been discovered on this site. The mines must have been known locally in the Middle Ages, but they were re-discovered by a clergyman in the 1870's. So put on the white helmet provided by the Department of the Environment and descend the iron ladder and see the flint-bearing chalk for yourselves, remembering that our ancestors excavated these mines only by the light of primitive animal-fat candles.

Hadleigh, *Suff,* (Tour 1). One of the many Suffolk towns once very prosperous in the woollen trade in the 16th century, Hadleigh retains a number of timber-framed houses. However, the two most interesting buildings are in the churchyard: first a timber-framed guildhall going back to the 15th century and now used for church activities, and second the 15th-century Deanery Tower. It is all that remains of the deanery, but it an impressive relic, with its two panelled octagonal corner towers, stepped battlements and 19th-century star-topped chimneys behind. The church has a 70-foot tall lead-covered spire built on top of the 64-foot tower. And outside the tower there is an unusual 13th-century clock bell. Inside the church is a grim brass commemorating the death of Rowland Taylor, a Protestant martyr burnt at the stake in 1555. Another sombre relic is a bench end in the south aisle depicting St Edmund's head held by a wolf – you will in fact see several more illustrations of that theme in other Suffolk churches. (See Bury St Edmunds.)

Happisburgh, *Norf,* (Tour 5). They all say this is pronounced 'Haisboro', and certainly from the awful number of sailors buried in the churchyard 'Happysborough' would hardly sound appropriate. The dead include 119 men lost when *HMS Invincible* was wrecked in 1801, all hands on *HMS Hunter* wrecked in 1804 and three German airmen from the Second World War. The church has a 110-foot high tower and an intriguing octagonal font.

Harwich, *Essex.* Though tourists travel through in their thousands on their way to the Continent, they seldom visit

Harwich. Built on a narrow site bordering on the huge estuaries of the Orwell and the Stour, Harwich has a long history of development and decline. It received its Charter in the 14th century, when it was a walled town. A royal dockyard was established here in the 17th century but was later supplanted by Sheerness. The train-ferry pier was built in 1924. The town has four main streets: King's Head Street has many interesting old buildings: number 14 has a wall painting and a plaster mural of a Tudor knight, number 21 is distinguished by a plaque telling us that this was the house of Captain Christopher Jones of the *Mayflower*.

Haslingfield, *Cambs,* (Tour 12) is well worth a visit. It has a mixture of thatched cottages and newer houses and stands below a 200-foot hill – quite a mountain for Cambridgeshire. The church font is 15th century and two figures in the vestry window are 14th century. The chancel roof must be unique – it was painted by a Victorian vicar.

*****Haughley Park,** *Suff,* (Tour 11) is an imposing Elizabethan manor house built in red brick in the 1620's, with five crow-stepped gables on the east front. Part of the interior was damaged in a fire in 1961 but it has been restored in style, including a six-foot wide oak staircase. Most of the paintings on view are 17th-century Dutch. There are attractive woods and gardens.

Heacham, *Norf.* As you will be informed by the village sign, Heacham was the home of the Rolfe family whose ancestor, John Rolfe, married the Indian Princess Pocahontas in 1614. She died young but left a son Thomas who went to Virginia and is related to the Gays, Giffords, Bollings, Murrays and Robertsons – or so we are told! Caley Mill, near the village, is the centre of the lavender industry, a delightful area if you are about when it is in bloom.

Helmingham, *Suff,* (Tour 2). Helmingham Hall itself is not open to the public but its gardens are. It is interesting to know that the moated 16th-century hall has been in the possession of the Tollemache family for 400 years. Originally a timber-and-brick building, it was spoilt to some degree in the 18th century, but made to look Tudor again in the 19th century. The draw-bridge is still raised every night. The gardens, with ornamental waterfowl and a variety of animals may be enjoyed by children. The church is full of monuments to the Tollemaches, nearly all of whom seem to have been called Lionel.

Helmingham Hall

Hingham, *Norf,* is best known for its connections with the Hingham in the USA. The Massachusetts Hingham was founded by a rector of the Norfolk town who had a dispute with the English church over his form of Puritanism. Another American connection is that Edward Lincoln came to Hingham and apprenticed his son Samuel to a weaver there – the weaver later left for the American Hingham, taking young Samuel with him. His descendant was Abraham Lincoln. Hingham has fine Georgian houses and the much-restored church has many attractions, including a hammerbeam roof.

The monuments include a huge red-stone memorial of Lord Morley, Baron of Rye and Marshal of Ireland, who died in 1434. It is thought that it may have been designed by the same man who created Erpingham Gate in Norwich.

Hintlesham, *Suff,* (Tour 1) has a charming Early English church, the nave and chancel being the oldest remaining parts. In the north aisle there is an unusual memorial to Captain John Timperley, carved in black stone with a white inlay to give the effect of a brass. The rood-screen decoration includes a number of grotesque heads. The Timperley family built the nearby Hintlesham Hall (not open to the public) in the 16th century, but the original Tudor façade is hidden by a later one erected in Georgian times.

*****Holkham Hall,** *Norf,* (Tour 8) is one of the finest Palladian houses in Britain and stands as a memorial to a remarkable family. Thomas Coke, 1st Earl of Leicester went on the Grand Tour of Italy in the early 1700's, met Lord Burlington and the architect William Kent and, having acquired a great hoard of statuary, pictures and books, set about building a house on the Holkham estate, which had been bought by the family some 100 years previously, to display them. Unhappily, he lived to see only part of the house built; the work took from 1734 until 1759, and he died in 1754. The estate went to a nephew and

then to his son, another Thomas Coke who, through his agricultural interests became famous as 'Coke of Norfolk'. He
pursued ideas on the rotation of crops and introduced new
breeds of sheep and cattle. On his death his neighbours erected
the great column to his memory which stands to the north of
Holkham Hall.

The exterior of the hall has been described as austere; its
features are classical certainly but its yellowish brick does not
match the colour of the Roman Renaissance brick it emulates.
However, the interior is superb: the great hall gleams with
colonnades of marble decorated with gold – William Kent
modelled this on the design of a Roman basilica. The north
dining room is shaped as a perfect cube and has a ceiling
designed by Inigo Jones. There is statuary there and also in the
statue gallery and North and South Tribune (these three rooms
are over 100 feet long). The landscape room has a collection of
Claude Lorrains as well as pictures by Poussin. The grounds,
laid out by Capability Brown, have a famous collection of trees,
including many ilex (cuttings of which go to feed the giraffes at
the London Zoo!).

Huntingdon, *Cambs,* (Tour 12) was the birthplace in 1599 of
Oliver Cromwell and both he and Samuel Pepys, the diarist,
went to the grammar school, now the *Cromwell Museum. In
the main street is Cromwell House, in which the Protector was
born; the records of his birth and baptism are preserved in the
nearby All Saints' church. The town has several pleasant
Georgian houses and the George Inn is of interest for its
galleried yard.

*Ickworth House,** *Suff,* (Tour 11) (NT) is reached from the
village of Horringer, where stand the gates to Ickworth Park.
The house is concealed by trees and one suddenly comes upon
its enormous presence – an 18th-century neo-classical building
with an imposing central rotunda housing a collection of works
or art as sumptuous as the building. The 100-foot high rotunda
is connected by a curved corridor to the two main wings.
Building started in 1796 and the house remained in the Hervey
family until 1956, when it was taken on by the National Trust.

The Herveys inherited the manor of Ickworth in 1485 and a
Hervey was created Earl of Bristol in 1714 for supporting the
Protestant Succession. The house was started by the Fourth
Earl Frederick Augustus Hervey, who was also a Bishop. He
travelled extensively in Europe purchasing many of the works
of art seen in the house, but he was captured by Napoleon's
troops in Italy in 1798 and lost all the precious objects he had
with him at the time. He saw the beginning of the building of 61

Ickworth but died in Italy in 1803, long before its completion. The Fifth Earl completed the east wing of the house, living there and entertaining in the rotunda – the reverse of his father's plan, which was to live in the rotunda and house his art collection in the wings. You enter the house by the huge Ionic portico, to be confronted by a group of statuary by Flaxman, who also created the illustrations to Homer which form the basis of the designs for the frieze in terracotta relief running round the outside cupola. The many Hervey portraits throughout the house are by Kneller, Lawrence, Romney, Gainsborough (a local artist), Reynolds and Grant.

Other works are by Velasquez and Hogarth. But perhaps the collection of Bristol silver, said to be one of the finest private collections in Britain, will attract most visitors; younger folk may be more interested in the collection of children's toys. The grounds, landscaped by Capability Brown, include a deer park and formal gardens.

Ipswich, *Suff,* (Tours 1 and 2). Ipswich is often compared unfavourably with Norwich. Although of ancient origin, Ipswich has destroyed much of its older architecture because commercial interests in the 19th century and the present one were so keen to modernize the town. However, there are still plenty of historic buildings to see if you know where to look and even some of the modern developments are of interest. Ipswich is also a good centre for touring.

Its situation on the wide River Orwell is something like London's relationship to the Thames, in that it is at the limit of navigability for large ships. (The river is called the Gipping in its upper reaches, and the town derives its name from the Anglo-Saxon Gipeswic.) Saxons and Danes invaded Ipswich from the sea and the town was a borough before the Norman Conquest, being granted a charter by King John in 1199. It reached its peak of importance as an entrepôt for the flourishing woollen trade in Suffolk during the 16th century, when wool towns like Lavenham sent their produce through Ipswich to the Continent. Cardinal Wolsey was born here, his father being a butcher and cloth merchant. Wolsey planned to build a College of Secular Canons here (in conjunction with his other foundation, Christ Church, Oxford). The building was actually started in 1528 but then Wolsey fell from power and all that remains is the brick gateway in College Street.

After the decline of the wool trade Ipswich became a shipping centre for goods such as coal, brought from Newcastle, and a boat-building centre. Then there was further decline until the 19th century, when the huge Wet Dock was built. Ipswich then became an industrial centre, famous for its engineering works, its manufacture of agricultural machinery, fertilizers and printing works. (Arthur Ransome, the author of children's adventure books was related to the Ransome lawn-mower manufacturers of Ipswich.) Most of these industries continue today, as you will observe.

If you are a family group, Ipswich is the sort of place where it may be best to split up and explore separately – the docks in particular may interest the fathers and sons more than the mothers and daughters.

The *Ancient House or Sparrowe's House, in the Butter-market, must be seen. Parts of it date back to the 15th century and the pargetting on the oriel windows is both elaborate and unusual; it represents all the continents as then known: Europe, Africa, Asia and America, as well as having the royal arms of Charles II. The Sparrowe family lived here from the 16th to the 19th century; as may be guessed they were staunch Royalists. The house is now an excellent bookshop. You may inspect some of the interior, which has good panelling and plasterwork ceilings together with an attractive courtyard. The front of the Ancient House is shown on the cover of this book.

Leaving the Buttermarket by Queen Street, you will come to Friar Street and see the Old Meeting House. Built in 1699 by a carpenter, Joseph Clarke, this wooden church has four great wooden pillars which are said to have been ships' masts, fine pews and galleries – in fact a study of craftsmanship in wood. Originally Presbyterian, the church became Unitarian at the end of the 18th century and remains so.

Ipswich has two good museums: the first, *Ipswich Museum in High Street, has a wonderful collection of archaeological specimens, particularly from the Early Stone Age, also a good collection of birds and animals. There are also replicas of the fascinating treasures from the Sutton Hoo Viking burial ship, the originals being in the British Museum (see p16).

The second museum, *Christchurch Mansion, stands in a park at the top of Northgate. The house is on the site of the Priory of the Holy Trinity and building began in 1548, although it was rebuilt in the 17th century after a fire. In the 1890's it was proposed to pull the place down and build a housing estate there! Fortunately for Ipswich and its many visitors, the Cobbold brewing family bought it and bequeathed it and the lovely park to the town. It contains a fine collection of furni-ture, a room used by Elizabeth I on her two visits there, a memorial to Wolsey and many pictures by Suffolk artists.

There is also an interesting collection of documents concerning Margaret Catchpole. This remarkable woman, born in 1773, was a servant with the Cobbold family. She fell in love with the son of a boatman and, the affair being frowned on by her family, she stole one of her master's horses to ride to London to see him. For that crime she was sentenced initially to death – later this was commuted to lifelong deportation, but she managed to escape from Ipswich prison. One of the handbills seeking her recapture may be seen in the museum. She was soon recaptured and sent to Australia where, after serving a few years imprisonment, she married and had three children. Another odd exhibit is the stuffed lyre bird she sent home to Mrs Cobbold. Richard Cobbold wrote a three-volume book about her life, said to contain 'many adornments'.

In Tavern Street you may see the great White Horse Inn where Mr Pickwick had his 'disconcerting experience with the lady in yellow curl papers'.

Down near the docks you will find Fore Street which has several old merchants' houses combining living accommodation with shops at the front and warehouses onto the river at the rear – they are similar to ones you may later see at King's Lynn. Note the Customs House here also – it was built in 1844 in a fine classical style, with a double staircase leading to a doorway sheltered by a pillared and pedimented portico.

Ixworth, *Suff,* (Tour 9) is a pleasant little town, with Tudor houses and a church dating from the 14th century, with a 16th-century hammerbeam roof. In the chancel is the tomb of Richard Coddington, who was given Ixworth in exchange for his manor at Cuddington in Surrey, where Henry VIII wanted originally to build Nonesuch Palace. Ixworth Abbey is now occupied by a school – the building contains some of the ancient priory of the 12th century, but all very mixed up with later additions.

Kersey, *Suff,* (Tour 1) was once a woollen manufacturing village and gave its name to a kind of cloth. It is a picturesque place, seen best from the church up the hill. That building is unusual in that its tower is completely of flint. The south porch has a wooden panelled ceiling – its rich ornamentation was covered for many years, being rediscovered in 1927. The roof of the nave has hammerbeams; there was a rood screen here in the 15th century and painted figures can be seen still on the six surviving panels.

Kessingland, *Suff,* (Tour 4) – see Suffolk Wildlife and County Park.

King's Lynn, *Norf,* (Tour 8) is a fascinating ancient town with reminders everywhere of its great trading past and the smell of the sea (although it isn't quite facing the sea, but on the Great Ouse). It is a great town to walk about, discovering old buildings and churches down almost every street.

About 1100 the first Bishop of Norwich founded St Margaret's church and the adjacent priory, endowing it with local lands. The town was 'Bishop's Lynn' until Henry VIII confiscated church property and it became King's Lynn. It was almost inevitable for the town to become a great trading port in the early Middle Ages: the produce of Norfolk, Cambridgeshire, Lincolnshire and the East Midlands were brought here by water – the wheat and wool – and the more exotic imports of furs and wines came back and travelled up the same inland waterways, making the Lynn merchants happy and prosperous. (You may still see their splendid houses, built with their warehouses backing on to the water, in King Street and Queen Street.) Lynn suffered a setback in the 19th century when the railways took away some inland waterways trading; but in recent years shipping activities have revived and you may see evidence of the many ships from Germany, Holland and the Baltic countries on the quays. The small fishing vessels belong to local fisherman who harvest the Wash for shrimps, cockles and mussels.

You might like to start your tour of King's Lynn at the Tuesday Market, going down Water Lane or Ferry Street to get a look at the waterside. The Market has several handsome buildings including the 17th-century Duke's Head and the 19th-century corn exchange. Going down nearby King Street you will come to *St George's Guildhall, the largest surviving medieval guildhall in England. It was once used as a theatre and it is known that Shakespeare's company played here, so he himself probably acted here also. The building has been used as a corn exchange and warehouse and was in some danger of demolition at one time, but a benefactor bought it and presented it to the National Trust, who still own it. It is now used as a theatre again and is the centre of King's Lynn's annual arts festival.

Further down King Street is the much-photographed Customs House; built in 1683 it has a statue of Charles II over the entrance. Crossing over into Queen Street you will see Clifton House, rebuilt in the 18th century but with an Elizabethan courtyard and an ancient warehouse at the back.

Another merchant's house, Hampton Court, will be seen further south in Nelson Street, complete with counting house. apprentices' quarters and warehouses; it has been restored by 65 the energetic King's Lynn Preservation Trust. Suspended from the roof of its entrance is a cannonball which was fired (it is said) by the Parliamentarians when besieging Lynn in 1643.

St Margaret's church, though founded in Norman times, as mentioned earlier, has little original surviving Norman fabric; there is a 13th-century chancel and a 15th-century clerestory. Over a window of the southwest tower is a rare clockwork moon dial which shows the phases of the moon and the times of high tide; it was restored to working order in 1969. The spire above this tower was blown down in a storm in 1741, badly damaging the nave and aisles. But the unique objects in the church are the two 14th-century brasses, Flemish work and both honouring mayors; Robert Braunche's brass is some nine feet long, while that of Adam de Walsoken is some ten feet long. The latter is decorated most copiously with over 100 figures and includes a pastoral scene with a representation of a post windmill, said to be the oldest illustration of such a mill. The Braunche memorial includes him and both his wives, all under canopies and protected by angels. At the base a banquet is depicted including a peacock, and some call this memorial the Peacock Feast. It may relate to the banquet given by Braunche to Edward III in 1349. Dr Burney, the organist at St Margaret's, was the father of the novelist Fanny Burney, who was born at Lynn in 1762.

Next we come to Saturday Market and Trinity Guildhall, with its chequered face of flint and freestone, built in 1421. It has no less than two royal coats of arms above the Elizabethan porch, the upper one taken from St James's church, demolished in 1559. The Guildhall's Regalia Room houses an extraordinary display of plate and records: there is a gold and enamel 'King John's Cup' and a 'King John's Sword'. (The town was given its first charter by King John in 1204.) Other charters since that date are displayed and also *The Red Book of Lynn* which details commercial relations between Lynn and Denmark, Iceland and other countries – Lynn men were prominent in the Greenland Whale Fishery.

Walking away from the river and crossing the busy St James Road you will come to The Walks: these are two lovely 18th-century avenues of lime and chestnut trees planted at right-angles to each other. They partly follow the old fortifications of the town, and a gateway made from the old town wall has been built where they meet. Nearby is the Red Mount Chapel. Built of red brick in 1485, it contains a lovely small chapel of stone, shaped like a cross and with marvellous fan-vaulting. It was said to have contained a relic of the Virgin Mary and was much visited by pilgrims in the 15th century. Speaking of pilgrimages, one is reminded of a famous Lynn lady who was a great pilgrim – Margery Kempe, writer of the first-ever biography in English. She was born in 1364, the daughter of a Mayor of King's Lynn. She married and had fourteen children and then went on pilgrimages to Jerusalem and Rome. Her book remained in a Lancashire library for 500 years until it was discovered in 1936. It is strange that a comparatively small place like King's Lynn was the birthplace of two women writers, Margery Kempe and Fanny Burney. But after your visit you may agree that Lynn is a strange and wonderful town and so a likely birthplace of writers.

Lavenham, *Suff,* (Tour 11). Lavenham (even its name is attractive) is so rich in timbered houses and has such a splendid church that no one should miss seeing it – but it is so popular that it often gets overcrowded. Nevertheless, if you can imagine the place when it was a quiet wool-weaving village – the loudest sound being the ringing of its famous church bells, you may enjoy its beauty even more. You will probably notice the *guildhall (NT) in Market Square first. It was built about 1530 by the Corpus Christi Guild. The carved corner posts of the porch are interesting; one depicts John de Vere, 15th Earl of Oxford (who gave Lavenham its charter). Another outstanding building is the Swan Inn, which now incorporates the old Wool Hall; the latter was almost destroyed 70 years ago – luckily it was rescued and restored by the Society for the Preservation of Ancient Buildings. Many other timbered houses with decorative pargetting will be seen in Church Street, Prentice Street and Shilling Street. (Shilling Grange in the latter Street was the home of Jane and Anne Taylor, who wrote songs for children, including the well-known *Twinkle, Twinkle, Little Star.)*

Lavenham's great church of St Peter and St Paul with its 140-foot tall tower of limestone and knapped flint was clearly built to rival the churches of other West Suffolk wool villages. The building was financed by the Earl of Oxford and the up-and-coming weaving families of Branch and Spring. It was in fact a re-building and took place at the end of the 15th and beginning of the 16th century. Thomas Spring's freshly received coat of arms occurs 32 times on the tower. The Earl of Oxford's de Vere arms similarly decorate the porch – which includes representations of wild boars, a pun on the de Vere name (*verres* is Latin for boar). It is revealing of the success of the mercantile families of that time to read that a niece of the Spring family married the 15th Earl of Oxford. The church's nave was added about 1513. Inevitably there is a Spring Chantry in the church; it has a splendid parclose screen of lovingly carved woodwork, thought to be of Flemish crafts-manship. The Branch Chapel contains many misericords decorated with uninhibited medieval imagery. We have men-tioned the church bells; the tenor bell weighs over a ton and is reputed to have the sweetest sound of any bell in England. A special peal is rung every year to celebrate the bell's 'birthday', the 21st June 1625.

On leaving Lavenham you may wonder at its unspoilt state. The truth is that the invention of power looms in areas which had waterpower at hand spelled the end of Lavenham's weav-ing industry. So, to our present day advantage, the village remained undeveloped, a monument to more prosperous times in the 16th century.

*__Layer Marney Tower,__ *Essex,* (Tour 3). Some may consider this 16th-century gatehouse a folly, for it was conceived as a grand entrance to a house that was never built because the Marney family became extinct! Nevertheless, it is a marvellous sight, the brick and terracotta towers rising in eight storeys to over 70 feet, the decoration having a very Italianate feeling. The place is open to the public one day a week, but you can see the gatehouse quite well from the nearby path to the church. The latter is worth looking into: opposite the octagonal pulpit is a 16th-century painting of St Christopher with Christ on his shoulders. There are also memorials to the Marneys, including that of Sir William Marney which stands inside six 16th-century wooden spiral posts linked by chains.

__Little Glemham,__ *Suff,* (Tour 2). The village church contains a remarkable monument to Dudley North and a brass which sheds light on the rude-sounding phrase 'Silly Suffolk' – the silly means holy, or wise:

> *'This sylly grave the ashes under hyde*
> *Of Thomas Glemham Sonn to Christopher.'*

*Glemham Hall is a fine 17th-century house, which some say looked even better before Dudley North (friend of Edmund Burke and an organizer of the trial of Warren Hastings) altered it in the 18th century. However, it has fine panelled rooms, family portraits and good Queen Anne furniture, together with large, attractive gardens.

__Little Maplestead,__ *Essex,* (Tour 3) is famous for having one of the five surviving round churches in England (another is in Cambridge). The village was given to the Knights of St John and Jerusalem in the 12th century – they had a duty to aid pilgrims travelling to the Holy Land and the round churches were built on the model of the church of the Holy Sepulchre in Jerusalem. Little Maplestead's church dates from about 1335 and may have been built on the site of an earlier one. The round 'aisle' is surrounded by an arcade of six pillars. There has been much 19th-century restoration – the west porch being of that period, but the west doorway is of an early date. The chancel has a painted timber roof.

Littleport, *Cambs,* (Tour 10) is not a very exciting place, but it has an interesting story in relation to the powers of the Bishops of Ely. In 1816 the farmworkers, many unemployed because of the enclosure of common land, marched to Ely and caused a disturbance, breaking some windows and frightening the citizens. The army were brought in and the Bishop of Ely appointed judges to make an example of the rioters, five of whom were hung and others transported. But this was the last exercise of the temporal power of the Bishop – a power originating in the tribal control of the Fens of a thousand years before. Littleport church is unusual in having two aisles and two naves – one of each being 15th century, the others 19th century.

Little Walsingham, *Norf,* (Tour 8). In 1061 Lady Richeldis, wife of the lord of the manor, had a vision of the Virgin Mary and afterwards built a shrine here. For centuries this became a place for pilgrimage, and every English king from Richard I to Henry VIII is said to have visited the shrine, many walking barefoot from Barsham Manor. The shrine was destroyed at the Dissolution of the Monasteries. The present one dates from 1931, and still attracts a great number of pilgrims. A priory was founded here by the Augustines in 1149; all that remains of that is the 15th-century east window standing in the abbey gardens.

Long Melford, *Suff,* (Tour 11), as its name implies, has an unusually long High Street, described as one of the finest village streets in England. It has many Tudor houses, together with 18th and 19th century ones, and is particularly attractive as it widens and becomes fringed by tree-shaded greens. At the north end stands *Melford Hall (NT) a fine Elizabethan house. It is thought that it originally was used as a hunting lodge by the Abbots of Bury St Edmunds before the Reformation. After that event it came into the hands of William Cordell, an ambitious man who rose to become Speaker of the House of Commons and served both Mary and Elizabeth, entertaining the latter Queen to an enormous banquet at Melford Hall in 1578 during a Royal Progress. The hall came down to the Parkers in 1786 and the eleventh Baronet still lives there. Many of the Parkers served in the navy and the present Baronet has a collection of old navigational instruments. The hall stands on three sides of a square and has medieval vaults. The bricks of the house were made from clay dug up in Melford Green nearby. The grounds are attractive with interesting topiary work and a Tudor garden pavilion.

Long Melford's Church of the Holy Trinity dominates the High Street and is superb. It was almost entirely rebuilt in Late Perpendicular style towards the end of the 15th century and has no less than 97 windows – the unusual proportion of glass to stone produces a 'floating' effect in the 150-foot long nave and chancel. The glass in the north aisle is of interest – it was originally Flemish work and has been restored. In the north wall see also a beautiful 14th-century sculpture in alabaster relief of the Adoration of the Magi. The Clopton aisle leads to the Clopton Chantry, passing through a small priest's room complete with fireplace, in which once lived a chantry priest devoted to saying masses for the Clopton family. The chantry contains a painted Easter tomb and the east window has a small but moving Lily Crucifix, a depiction of the Lily of the Annunciation in which the Crucifixion can be seen. The Lady Chapel, although a separate building, can be reached from the body of the church: it is encircled by a unique indoor cloister.

Long Stratton, *Norf,* (Tour 7). St Mary's church has a number of curiosities. Its tower is round but, as mentioned earlier, that is not very unusual in East Anglia. The church clock has only one hand and inside the church on the north aisle wall is a 15th-century 'sexton's wheel' used to determine the day on which a course of prayers should start.

Lowestoft, *Suff,* (Tour 4) geographically is not unlike Yarmouth, with Oulton Broad behind the town instead of Breydon Water. The town is part fishing port and part holiday resort. Its maritime importance developed in the 19th century, when the inner and outer harbour were built and the railway reached the town enabling fish to be transported quickly to Billingsgate. The fish harbour is worth visiting – you may see kipper-curing houses and net drying. The town is divided by a swing bridge into north and south areas. The north side is the older, having old houses running down to the sea in alleys called 'scores'. St Margaret's church dates from the 15th century and has a restored hammerbeam roof. Both north and south areas have bathing beaches – the southern esplanade is pedestrianized and probably a safer place for children, the sea being shallow with a sand-and-shingle beach.

Lynn and Wensum Forests, *Norf,* (Tour 8). These are the collective names of 8 000 acres of woodlands situated in the northwest and northeast parts of Norfolk. Controlled by the Forestry Commission, they comprise some 50 small woods. As in other parts of East Anglia, the forests have been established on poor agricultural land. In contrast to the great pine-growing policy in Thetford Forest (see below) oak, red cedar and Lawson cypress were sown at Lynn and Wensum; they were not very successful however and the Corsican pine now predominates, but many of these broad-leaved trees still survive at the edge of forests in north Norfolk and they certainly are attractive. These comparatively young forests only produce some 60 000 cubic metres of small timber annually. Fallow deer may be seen in Wensum and white fallow deer in Lynn Forest. Grey squirrels are spreading also – difficult pests to control in forests close to much private land. Picnic places are provided at many of these woods and there are also some waymarked forest walks.

Madingley, *Cambs,* is a pleasant village on the edge of the park of Madingley Hall, a Tudor house now used by Cambridge University. The church of St Mary's is old, though much restored, a unique feature being the surviving 15th-century glass.

Maldon, *Essex,* is an ancient town situated on a hill overlooking the upper reaches of the river Blackwater. Like so many East Anglian towns with access to the sea it suffered attacks by the Danes in the 10th century – a great battle taking place south of the town in 991, when the Saxon king Ethelred was defeated. There are several houses dating from the 15th century in or near the High Street. The 13th-century All Saints' church is famous for its triangular tower, the only one in England. It contains two odd monuments inside: one to Edward Bright, who weighed 43 stone when he died in 1750 and another to Thomas Cammock, depicted with his two wives who bore him 22 children. He died in 1602. The 15th-century Moot Hall is a good example of brickwork of that date – it has a fine brick spiral staircase.

March, *Cambs,* (Tour 10). St Wendreda's church has a 16th-century double hammerbeam roof decorated with a magnificent panoply of wide-winged angels, said to be the finest in the country. The angels at the base of the wall posts carry different

71

musical instruments. The church has 13th-century beginnings, the aisles and clerestory being 15th century – but you probably won't observe much other than those marvellous angels!

Nayland, *Suff,* (Tour 1) was once a weaving town and you may see the old weavers' cottages with typical Suffolk pargetting. Near the church is Alston Court dating from the late 15th century, with Tudor additions. The ornate stone porch of St James' church was built by a cloth manufacturer William Abell in 1525 (later restored) – he also financed the bridge over the Stour nearby. John Constable painted the altar picture of *Christ Blessing the Elements.* Someone once criticized it because the figure resembled too closely the artist's brother, Golding!

North Walsham, *Norf,* (Tour 5) is an attractive market town – once a wool-weaving centre. The unusual market cross is octagonal with a roof supported by eight pillars above which are three domes like a wedding cake – it was built about 1600. The church of St Nicholas is one of the largest in Norfolk. There are the ruins of a tower, part of which fell down in the 18th century and more in the 19th! The chancel screen dado is decorated with paintings of 17 saints. Nearby is the huge monument to Sir William Paston, dressed in armour and reclining on one elbow. This church recalls an unhappy event after the Peasants' Revolt in 1381. The peasants attacked Norwich and killed the Commander of the City; the Bishop of Norwich led the attack against the peasants, who were defeated on North Walsham Heath. One of the leaders sought sanctuary in this church, but he was dragged outside and killed.

Norwich, *Norf,* (Tours 5, 6 and 7) was, for centuries, the second most important city in England. Because of its geographical position – with easier access to the Continent than London in earlier times – it has always had a unique character. It is proud of its past, retaining many of its ancient buildings because industrial development passed the city by – a city with its own local culture, its own school of painting, its own theatre and now its own university. The city is on a hill and the river Wensum winds round it like an elongated question mark. It is a difficult place to find your way about in – if you turn left twice you are back where you started – largely because of the many winding streets. There is a one-way traffic system which keeps traffic flowing but it not easy for a stranger to understand. Definitely a place to park your car (the large car park near the Castle Museum is an ideal starting point for wandering).

72   *History.* The Romans had a town nearby at Caistor St

Tombland Alley, Norwich

Edmunds, of which little now exists. Norwich became a town in the 9th century. After the Norman Conquest the castle was built on what was a natural hill, but one heightened from the moat digging. The bishop's throne was removed from Thetford to Norwich in 1094, being housed in the Saxon church then on the site of the cathedral, the building of which began two years later and lasted some hundreds of years. A market was established in the shadow of the castle and became the greatest in East Anglia. Local crafts flourished – tanning and leatherwork, metal founding and weaving. Later the manufacture of worsted cloth became a great industry, and the rich wool merchants of the 14th century built themselves fine houses and contributed towards the building of Norwich's many churches.

In the 16th century Belgian and Dutch refugees were welcomed to the town and brought with them new weaving skills. But, as has been said, Norwich's industrial importance faded when coal and water became an essential in the mechanization of production. It has now changed again and many local industries, shoemaking, printing, food manufacture (and insurance!) now flourish, albeit beyond the old town walls.

It is impossible to detail all the many attractions of the town, but here are the main ones.

*The Castle. A wooden castle was built on the present site soon after the Conquest, and the present stone keep was erected in the 12th century. It became neglected in the 14th century (when a city wall was built) and was restored by Salvin in the 1830's. It served as a prison until it became a museum in the 1890's. It is an informative place to visit before touring

Norfolk. The dioramas in the Norfolk room which explain the nature of the Broads, Breckland and other surrounding areas are particularly worthwhile. Then there is the art gallery, with rooms devoted to the Norwich School of Crome and Cotman (see p22). There is also a unique collection of teapots in one gallery – appropriately not far from the snack bar! The Norfolk Museums Service has high standards and you will enjoy other museums under its jurisdiction during your tour of Norfolk.

From the castle you may walk along the pedestrianized shopping streets to Norwich's famous Market Place – a large open place covered with colourful awnings. St Peter Mancroft stands above the market, with the huge city hall in the centre, and to the right the 15th-century guildhall. St Peter Mancroft should not be missed (it looks lovely when floodlit at night, as do many other of Norwich's buildings). It is 15th century and Perpendicular in style with huge clear windows which make it unusually light inside. The east window, with stained glass mostly of the 15th century, is very fine. There is a hammerbeam roof but the hammerbeams are concealed by fan-vaulting. *Elm Hill,* a cobbled street with many timbered houses, is probably the most photographed part of Norwich. It now houses many antique shops.

St Peter Hungate Museum on the corner of Elm Hill and Princes Street is a 15th-century church, now turned into a museum of Norfolk ecclesiastical art.

The Bridewell Museum is a wealthy merchant's house of the 14th century now a museum specializing in local industries such as spinning and weaving, shoe manufacture and local building methods.

Strangers' Hall in Charing Cross street is not far away, housing a museum of a different kind: its rooms show the furniture and utensils of different periods. The house itself is 15th century but the undercroft is thought to be of the 13th.

The Maddermarket Theatre is behind Strangers' Hall. It was converted into an Elizabethan-style theatre in the 1920's and has the reputation of being the best amateur theatre in England.

The Cathedral. The then Bishop of East Anglia, Herbert de Losinga, began the building of the cathedral in 1096; he completed the presbytery and transepts but died in 1119. More Norman work is evident here than in almost any other cathedral in Britain, but because of the collapse of a spire and a later fire it is mainly the supporting Norman arches which remain. The upper gatehouse, the Ethelbert Gate, leads you into a quiet close, which was once the monastic part of the precinct. Entering by the west door you will immediately be impressed by the great length of the nave. The 15th-century vaulted roof is embellished with many detailed bosses representing incidents from the Bible. The choir contains canopied stalls of the 15th century with many amusing misericords under the seats.

You will notice that the presbytery is higher than the nave. The Norman arches support the 14th-century clerestory and above that a 15th-century vault, again with many interesting bosses. At the east end is the ancient bishop's throne, restored in recent years but embodying two stones which have been dated as 8th century, thought to have originated at the earlier cathedral of East Anglia at North Elmham. Passing round the ambulatory you come to St Luke's chapel, which houses a 14th-century retable depicting five scenes from the New Testament.

The cloister is the largest in Britain: the east walk is 14th century and decorated, the north 15th and Perpendicular. Again many bosses are to be seen, and here closer to your eyes!

Outside the cathedral you may wonder at the central Norman tower ornamented with tiers of arcading and decorative circles with the 15th-century spire above. Norwich is proud of its cathedral – and has every reason to be.

Walking down from the grassed Upper Close to the Lower Close you find a lane leading to Pull's Ferry. It is a 15th-century

The Priory Watergate 'Pull's Ferry', Norwich

water-gate to the cathedral precinct – a reminder of the times when it was easier to travel about Norfolk by water than by road. (Pull was the name of an 18th-century ferryman, we are told).

The places described above are in the area of the castle and cathedral, south of the Wensum river. If you walk north of the 75 river along George Street or Duke Street you will find the following.

Gurney's Court, discovered through a small entry from Magdalen Street, is completely Georgian in character. It is noteworthy because Elizabeth Gurney was born in the corner house in 1780. She is known to the world as Elizabeth Fry, the zealous prison reformer. Oddly enough another woman of character was born in the same house twenty years later – the writer Harriet Martineau.

The Old Meeting House stands behind a forecourt on the other side of Magdalen street from Gurney's Court. Built in the 17th century, this was first a Unitarian and then a Congregational church. Inside, there are galleries on three sides and pews all facing a prominent high pulpit.

St Michael's Church stands at the end of Colegate Street. Built about 1500, the eastern exterior exhibits one of the finest examples of stone flushwork in the county – you will see that whole window patterns and their tracery are outlined in alternating flint and stone. On the west door the tracery is of later workmanship, being designed by the local artist Cotman.

Orford, *Suff,* (Tour 2) is one of the many towns in East Anglia which was once an important port – in fact from Elizabethan times until the 17th century – its waters became too shallow, partly because of silting and partly because ships got bigger! From the top of *Orford Castle you may observe the strange process of the River Ore. As the River Alde it almost reaches the sea at Aldeburgh but then turns southwards running parallel to the coastline and is then called the Ore, reaching the sea at Hollesly Bay. The castle was built for Henry II from 1165 to 1172. Originally, there was a keep set in a bailey and surrounded by a curtain wall which, unusually for its period, had a number of defensive towers spread along it so that defenders could discharge arrows against any attackers who had gained the wall. The keep is the only surviving part. It is circular in section, although the exterior is polygonal, and had three additional towers set equidistant around it. Standing 90 feet high, the keep has walls ten feet thick and is divided into three storeys. The castle was built partly to oppose the powerful Hugh Bigod, Earl of Norfolk, who, in fact, led a rebellion against the King almost as soon as the castle was completed. The rebellion was crushed and Orford remained an important part of the crown's controlling power in East Anglia for many years.

Orford's large parish church is mainly 14th century and has a ruined Norman chancel nearby. Several of Benjamin

Britten's works had their first performance in this church during the annual Aldeburgh Festival.

Oulton, *Norf,* (Tour 4) is the centre of one of the busiest boating places, Oulton Broad being the most southerly of the Broads. The writer George Borrow once lived here. If you happen to visit when the annual carnival is held here in the summer, you will see a splendid firework display held at the edge of the water.

Over, *Cambs,* (Tour 8) has an outstanding church dating from the 14th century whose features include unusual gargoyles, a sculpture of Our Lady in Glory on the south porch and a sanctus bell in a turret over the eastern gable of the nave. The ancient misericords within were taken from Ramsey Abbey.

Oxburgh Hall

*Oxburgh Hall, Norf, (Tour 9) (NT) is at Oxborough (the house seems to have always had the shorter spelling). It was built in 1482 by Sir Edmund Bedingfield and Bedingfields still live there today. The family was both loyalist and Catholic and therefore lost favour with the Crown after the Reformation, suffering for their loyalty at the hands of the largely Cromwellian East Anglians.

The most striking feature on first viewing the hall is the fortified gatehouse across the wide moat which surrounds it. Pugin called it 'one of the noblest specimens of the domestic architecture of the 15th century'. Instead of a drawbridge, an 18th-century bridge crosses the moat. The hall appears more like a castle, but in fact many of the defensive features such as the arrow slits in the towers and the machicolations were purely decorative. Inside the gatehouse is a wonderful spiral staircase made of brick, not stone, and a memorial to Norfolk bricklayers of that time. The King's Chamber houses the famous Oxburgh Hangings: these green velvet wall hangings were sewn by Mary Queen of Scots during her long imprisonment, aided by the faithful 'Bess of Hardwick'; there are over a hundred panels representing animals and plants. Oxburgh retains its original ground-plan but there have been some losses: the Tudor Hall and Great Chamber which once stood opposite the gatehouse were demolished in 1775, leaving the south side of the once enclosed courtyard open to the moat.

Parham, *Suff,* (Tour 2) is a picturesque village with a thatched vicarage and a windmill. The 16th-century Parham Hall (not open to the public) is now a farm – an unusual one in that it is enclosed by a moat. The bells of the parish church hang in their original 14th-century frame.

St Nicholas' Church, Potter Heigham

Potter Heigham, *Norf,* is a popular Broadland centre, 11 miles northwest of Great Yarmouth on the A149, which passes over a three-arched medieval bridge. The village of Potter Heigham is a mile to the north of that picturesque bridge: its church has a round tower with an octagonal belfry 500 years old. The church font is unusual in that it is built of brick; there are also some early wall paintings.

Ramsey, *Cambs,* is now the centre of an important vegetable-growing area, but it was once the site of a great Benedictine abbey, founded in 969. The later Lady Chapel of the abbey is now incorporated into the Abbey Grammar School (not open to the public), but you may visit the 15th-century gatehouse (NT).

Reedham, *Norf,* is an attractive waterside village with several hospitable public houses. Nearby is Reedham chain ferry, the only means between Norwich and Great Yarmouth of getting a car across the Yare river.

Saffron Walden, *Essex,* is an old market town, once one of the most important in the country. The name Walden derives from Wealas, the word from which the term 'Welsh' came and means 'the valley of the Britons'. The Saffron relates to the saffron industry which flourished here in the middle ages and up to the 18th century. (Saffron is the dried orange stigma of the saffron crocus used as a dye, in medicine and also in cookery.) There was a Saxon settlement here; the Normans built a castle on the low ridge now in the centre of the town. The wool and saffron industries flourished in the 14th and 15th centuries, during which time many of the fine houses and the church were built.

Many of the best houses are in the High Street. On the corner of Middylton Place is a beautiful Tudor timbered house, now belonging to the Youth Hostel Association. More fine houses are in George Street and Church Street, some of them with pargetting. Only the keep of the castle remains: it was built about 1100 by Geoffrey de Mandeville.

St Mary's church is one of the largest in Essex. It was built in the second half of the 15th century on the site of a cruciform 13th-century church in an unusual style for Essex. The architect was John Wastell, the master mason of King's College chapel at Cambridge (see under Cambridge) with which St Mary's displays some affinities – notably the octagonal turrets at the east corner of the nave. The exterior is mostly of the local hard chalk called clunch, plus the inevitable flint to be found in this part of England. The interior is impressive because of the width of the aisle and the height of the walls, enhanced by the large clerestory windows. The north chapel houses a tomb-chest of John Leche, vicar at the time the church was built, who died in 1521. In the south chapel is the tomb of Lord Thomas Audley, Henry VIII's Lord Chancellor, rendered in a black stone, called touch. (See under Audley End.)

There is an intriguing maze on the common, east of the market place. A pattern is cut in the turf in the shape of a large and smaller circles. It is thought that this may be a pre-Christian relic.

St Ives, *Cambs,* (Tour 12) takes its name from St Ivo, a Persian missionary-bishop after whom a priory was dedicated here in 1050. A medieval bridge spans the Ouse, unusually having a chapel in its centre bay. Oliver Cromwell was a churchwarden in the 15th-century All Saints' church – he farmed nearby for five years – and a statue to him stands in Market Hill. *The Norris Museum contains a collection of local relics and manuscripts including an example of a very early ice skate used by those famous Cambridgeshire skaters who were able to skate every winter when the Great Ouse froze over.

St Neots, *Cambs,* (Tour 12) is on the Great Ouse, and one side of its market place actually backs on to the wide river. The town goes back a thousand years, but the oldest remaining building is the splendid 15th-century parish church, which has a richly decorated tower and intriguing carvings of animals, angels and birds on the roof inside.

Sandringham Park, *Norf,* (Tour 8) covers 7 000 acres of woodland and heathland surrounding the royal residence of Sandringham House. Bought by the Prince of Wales in 1861, parts are maintained as a country park and, when the Royal Family is not in residence, the *gardens may also be visited. The main gates to the park are a splendid example of 19th-century ironwork. You may attend services at Sandringham's parish church, as long as local parishioners have seats. It has been much restored and contains several gold and silver items given by an American, Mr Rodman Wanamaker, who once lived near Sandringham.

Saxtead Green, *Suff,* (Tour 2) is famous for its post mill, dating from the 18th century but with a superstructure rebuilt in 1859. The whole body of the mill is built on a single central post and is turned by the fantail to take the wind, the weight being taken on wheels which run around the circular track at the base. It is in charge of the Department of the Environment.

Snape, *Suff,* (Tour 2) on the river Alde, is best known now for the malting works, which fell into disuse in 1965 when part of the buildings was converted into a concert hall for use during the annual Aldeburgh music festival. (See above.) From Snape you may tread the five mile 'Sailor's Walk' along the north bank of the Alde all the way to Aldeburgh.

*****Somerleyton Hall,** *Suff,* (Tour 4). An Elizabethan mansion, it was enlarged and rebuilt by Samuel Morton Peto (after making a fortune from the railways) in 1846. Opinions differ as to the 'restoration' but it does contain superb tapestries, pictures and carvings. The extensive grounds have a maze, a children's farm, nature trails and a miniature railway. Mr Peto also rebuilt the village of Somerleyton, complete with thatched cottages.

Southend-on-Sea, *Essex.* A more accurate name would be Southend-on-the-Thames-Estuary, but one could hardly expect the enterprising folk who developed the 'south end' of Prittlewell village into a great popular resort, mainly for the entertainment of Londoners, to call it by such a prosaic mouthful! Its development began at the end of the 18th century and the town was honoured in 1801 when Princess Charlotte visited it to take a course in sea bathing. Two years later her mother Caroline, Princess of Wales, stayed at the Terrace, which was there upon re-named Royal Terrace. By 1870 the population of Southend had increased to 3 000 and then in the next 40 years to 70 000, since when it has doubled again. The town now embraces the former villages of Shoebury, Southchurch, Prittlewell, Eastwood and Leigh-on-Sea.

Southend's popularity was at its peak before the Second World War when few people owned cars and it could be reached easily by train or coach from London. It has now developed as a commuter town, although a great many new offices have been built in recent years, including some for Government Departments.

The pier, over a mile long and said to be the longest in the world, was built in 1890 and lengthened in 1930. There is little of architectural interest in the town but at Prittlewell are the remains of a 12th-century Cluniac priory: the refectory, cellars and cloister garth remain in what is now a public park. A 19th-century wing to the priory houses the South-East-Essex Museum. A 16th-century manor house may be found in Southchurch road, with a finely-panelled great hall. Southend takes a lot of trouble with its many public gardens – the quietest area is probably Westcliff, where the promenade really does have a seaside atmosphere because of the modest cliffs you find there.

South Walsham, *Norf,* (Tour 6). The village has an interesting church with 15th-century features, but most visitors will be concerned with the unique *Fairhaven Garden Trust at South Walsham. This woodland garden, created largely by Lord Fairhaven, covers 174 acres and surrounds the South Walsham Inner Broad. Shade and water-loving plants and shrubs have been encouraged, and there are camellias and rhododendrons specially imported from the Himalayas. There is also a bird sanctuary, for which prior arrangement is needed for a visit.

Southwold, *Suff,* (Tour 4) built almost on an island, is an unspoilt seaside town. Once a prosperous fishing port, it was badly damaged by a fire in 1659 – the burnt-down areas were left without buildings, giving Southwold no less than seven greens. In 1672 the battle of Sole Bay was fought out between the British and Dutch navies, the townspeople watching the awful event from the cliff tops. Some 800 wounded were brought ashore at Southwold.

The town has many pleasing Georgian houses, but its main glory is the church of St Edmund. Built in the Perpendicular style in the 15th century, there is rich flushwork particularly on the south side and on the 100-foot west tower. The 16th-century chancel screen, on which twelve assorted angels and saints can be seen, is one of the finest painted screens in the country. Then there is an intriguing Jack o' the Clock, an armoured figure of the 15th century which strikes the clock with an axe at every hour (he is called Southwold Jack). The superb 15th-century painted pulpit is very rare.

The largest of the greens, South Green, continues to Gun Hill, where six ancient cannons overlook the sea. They are said to have been captured by the Duke of Cumberland at Culloden and presented to the town.

Stanway Green, *Essex,* (Tour 3). *Colchester Zoo is in the grounds of Stanway Hall, three miles west of Colchester. Also in the 40-acre park are the ruins of All Saints' church, a 14th-century building much damaged during the Civil War.

Stoke-by-Nayland, *Suff,* (Tour 1). The church tower has been seen by millions of people who do not know its name, for this was the church Constable introduced into many of his landscapes, as well as painting a picture of the church itself. The church is in a lovely setting in a close of Tudor houses and surrounded by trees. The famous tower, topped by battlements and pinnacles, is 120 feet high. The south porch is in Decorated style and has noteworthy bosses in the roof. Inside, the soaring tower arch is impressive and there is wonderful carving everywhere – note particularly the frieze of angels and flowers below the clerestory windows. In the south chancel are brass memorials to Lady Tendring and Sir William Tendring (a six-foot brass to him). Their daughter married a Howard – hence the many Tendring and Howard arms seen about the church – and they were the ancestors of both Lady Catherine Howard and Anne Boleyn, wives of Henry VIII. Two fine timbered houses near the church are the Guildhall and the Maltings. Two miles south of Stoke-by-Nayland is Thorington Hall, built about 1600, but it is only open to National Trust members on application to the tenant.

Stowmarket, *Suff,* (Tour 11). This market town and agri-cultural centre of central Suffolk has an interesting *Museum of East Anglian Life, exhibiting all sorts of articles, many of them shown out of doors, relating to the rural life of the area. There are also several ancient buildings which had been in danger of destruction but have now been removed and re-erected here. The museum stands on the site of a rest-house belonging to the Abbots of St Osyth in the 14th and 15th centuries. Stowmarket's church is noteworthy for its timbered spire.

Stretham, *Cambs,* (Tour 10) is a pleasant village with several Georgian houses. A three-storied pumping house on the bank of the river houses a beam engine, a rare example of a pumping engine used for fen drainage; it once lifted water at the rate of 124 tons a minute. To the north of the village is a black tower windmill from which one may obtain a view of the distant Ely Cathedral.

Sudbury, *Suff,* (Tour 1), standing on the river Stour is the biggest of the Suffolk weaving towns, but different from the others in that weaving still goes on there, as well as other kinds of manufacturing. The Gainsborough Museum, his birthplace in Gainsborough Street, has some of his paintings as well as furniture of his period. A bronze statue to him stands on Sudbury Market Hill. (See also p20.)

St Gregory's church has a grim reminder of another of Sudbury's sons – the skull of Simon Tybald. He was Archbishop of Canterbury and Chancellor of England in Richard II's time. However, he antagonized the poor and Wat Tyler's rebels dragged him from the Tower of London (where he was hiding) and beheaded him.

Another of Sudbury's churches, St Peter's, has a 17th-century nave roof panelled in blue and gold and a famous piece of 15th-century embroidery on velvet, called the Sudbury Pall — and still used at the funerals of aldermen.

Sudbury was the model of Dickens' town of Eatanswill in *Pickwick Papers* and identifiable because he describes so well the 15th-century Salter's Hall in the town.

Suffolk Wildlife and Country Park, *Kessingland* (Tour 4). Situated on the A12 south of Lowestoft, the country park has a collection of animals including lions, tigers and monkeys; there is also a children's play area, and cafés.

Swaffham, *Norf,* (Tour 8) is a small market town with many 18th-century houses. In the market place is a little rotunda built of Tuscan pillars and supporting a figure of Ceres at the top of a   83

Market Cross, Swaffham

dome – it was built by Horace Walpole in 1783. The north aisle of the nearby church is supposed to have been built with monies provided by John Chapman, the Pedlar of Swaffham, who dreamt that there was treasure under a tree in his garden – which proved to be true! The Pedlar's dog appears in the south porch of the church and the Pedlar himself is seen in several carvings in the body of the church. Other attractions are a double hammerbeam roof and a host of angels.

Thaxted, *Essex,* is almost halfway between Saffron Walden and Great Dunmow on the A130. Like Lavenham and Long Melford in Suffolk, its 15th- and 16th-century houses and its fine church derive from its prosperity at that time due to weaving and, in the case of Thaxted, cutlery manufacture. After the Norman Conquest Thaxted manor was given to Richard de Clare.

Thaxted's High Street has houses of a variety of ages and it leads you to the wonder of the 15th-century guildhall, standing in the middle of the street. It has open arcades on the ground floor and two timbered storeys above under a double-gabled roof – in fact the structure looks over-heavy for its supporting timbers. In Watling Street near the guildhall is Beach House of the 17th century, after which your feet are then drawn to St John's church.

One of the grandest churches in Essex, its building began in about 1340. It is embattled all round, with pinnacles on chancel and aisles, with a solid tower at the west end surmounted by a graceful spire supported by flying buttresses (this spire replaced the original one destroyed by lightning a hundred years ago). The church has two porches, the King's and the

Duke's, the donors being Edward IV and the Duke of Clarence. Both porches are vaulted and have a spiral stair leading to a room above. Inside, the church with its graceful arches and light clerestory is impressive, partly because of its size – the north and south aisles are wider than the nave. The roof transepts are 14th century with carved timbers and ornamental bosses, the other roofs being 15th- and 16th-century work. There is a wealth of birch panelling everywhere.

Among the interesting items are a canopied oak pulpit dated 1680 and a font encased in wood with 15th-century carving. The glass includes 15th-century work and has four Garden of Eden scenes with bishops and angels. There is also much work of modern artists here in iron, glass and embroidery.

Thetford, *Norf,* (Tour 9). This charming little town clearly owed its beginnings to its strategic position at the meeting of two rivers, the Thet and the Little Ouse, the latter giving it water communication with King's Lynn. You may get a good view of the town by climbing Thetford Castle, reached across the meadow from Castle Street. It is simply a huge mound, or more correctly a motte. 100 feet high and of some 800 feet circumference, no mean effort to build with simple tools. It may date from the 8th century, but could even be the remains of an ancient Iron Age fort. It once had a parapet and wooden ramparts, but there is no trace of stone.

The marauding Danes were allowed to settle in Thetford in 866. The town exchanged hands over the years, but when the Danes had attained control of all East Anglia in 1012 King Sweyne made Thetford his capital, as later did King Canute. After the Norman Conquest the town again achieved eminence because it was made a bishopric and Great St Mary Church became a cathedral (later the bishopric was moved to Norwich).

In 1107 Henry I held his court in Thetford and laid the foundation stone of the Priory of Our Lady, which was founded by his friend Roger Bigod, Earl of Norfolk. Like the priory at Castle Acre (see above) it was of the Cluniac order. Little now remains to be seen except the foundations, the remains of the prior's lodgings and a 14th-century gatehouse. Mowbray and Howard, Dukes of Norfolk, were buried at the Priory, but after the Dissolution the remains of Thomas Howard, Duke of Norfolk, and of his wife and son were removed to Framlingham (see above). There are the remains of four other ecclesiastical foundations around the town.

*The Ancient House in White Hart Street is worth seeing, particularly as it now houses a museum. A 15th-century timbered house, it contains a fine carved-beam ceiling. The house was given to the town in 1921 by Prince Duleep Singh, who made his home in Norfolk. The collection includes many Stone Age implements found in surrounding Breckland.

St Peter's Church with Thomas Paine's Statue, Thetford

In the town opposite the famous half-timbered Bell Hotel and outside the Georgian King's House stands a statue to Thetford's most famous son (and the enemy of kings), Thomas Paine. He was born here in a house in White Hart Street in January 1737, the son of a Quaker staymaker and educated at the local grammar school, (which you may still see in the town). On the invitation of Benjamin Franklin, he visited America in 1774, writing *Common Sense*, a plea for American Independence two years later. He returned to England and published his *Rights of Man* in 1790. It sold 1½ million copies in England alone, an enormous number for that time. Threatened with a charge of sedition he went to France, where he wrote *The Age of Reason*. He died in America in 1809 but his remains were later brought back to England. The fine statue in Thetford was executed by Charles Wheeler, a one-time President of the Royal Academy. It was presented to Thetford by the Thomas Paine Society of the United States.

Thetford has suffered a series of ups and downs in its long history. In the early 1800's an attempt was made to turn it into a spa town. That failed, but fresh life was encouraged in 1845 with the coming of the railway – Thetford is on the London-Norwich line. And in recent years the town has become an overspill area for London.

Thetford is a pleasant place to walk from. You can stroll
along the banks of the Little Ouse through woodlands towards

Brandon – in fact, as far as Brandon, if you are energetic enough. (See Thetford Forest below.)

Thetford Forest, *Norf,* (Tour 9) some 80 square miles in area, and the second largest Forestry Commission property in Britain, is situated in Breckland, a large expanse of infertile sandy heathland with little agricultural use. It was acquired by the Commission in the early 1920's when rabbit farming was the only profitable activity (the pelts were used in the fur felt factories in Brandon). The newly-formed Forestry Commission planted the area with Scots and Corsican pines and now, over fifty years later with the huge trees stretching to the horizon, it is difficult to imagine the bare heathland which existed before. Three gently flowing rivers flow through the forest from east to west: the Wissey, the Little Ouse and the Lark. Scots pine was planted mainly because it can withstand the periods of drought and the spring and autumn frosts. Pine seedlings were raised in nurseries within the forest – some 200 acres of nursery land producing some seven million transplants annually. They were planted in 25 acre plots, with broad-leaved trees on the borders to prevent the spread of fire and also as an amenity – you will still see the mature broad-leaved trees beside the roads.

Much of the timber is processed at the Forestry Commission's depot near Brandon railway station, the largest conversion depot of its kind in Britain. The forest produces some 125 000 cubic metres of timber annually – expected to rise to 140 000 cubic metres by 1985. One sixth of the timber goes to the National Coal Board for pitprops. The felling and replanting programme is managed to ensure that no large area is denuded of trees. Corsican pines are being used now in replanting because they have been found to produce a much more economical timber yield. Natural regeneration is allowed to take place in some parts of the forest.

The forest is administered from the old village of Santon Downham (Tour 9) which has an information centre where you will obtain any advice you need about the facilities in the forest. Over a hundred of the Commission staff are housed at Santon, where also the radio-controlled fire tenders are maintained.

There are many picnic areas all over Thetford Forest. From most of these, forest walks are signposted, with generally one short and one longer walk. Then, there are some forest trails in areas of particular interest and for these booklets are provided pointing out the things to look out for on the way. For serious walkers there is a 23-mile route marked through the forest, but many middle distance walks are possible – for instance, along the tow-path following the Little Ouse from Brandon to Thetford with a break at Santon Downham; the Pilgrim's Walk from Weeting to Cranwich, or the Icknield Way from the King's Forest to the northern side of Lackford village.

The red squirrel is a species you are sure to meet in the forest. They are common here – one of their last major strongholds in the southern half of Britain. You may also see three species of deer, red, roe and fallow; a fourth species, the muntjac has also appeared (surprisingly, they are thought to have spread from Bedfordshire). It should be noted that the game in the forest is let out for shooting and that dogs must be kept on a leash to prevent them disturbing the game.

The low rainfall and continental type of climate in the Breckland area has meant that many rare plants grow here that are not seen anywhere else in Britain. Afforestation has diminished the numbers of plants to be seen, but they still exist on open heath and in the many forest rides and firebreak verges. In the spring you may see yellow and blue forget-me-nots, wall speedwell, rue-leaved saxifrage, spring vetch and the rare moonwort fern. The summer brings lady's bedstraw, wild mignonette, musk mallow, birdsfoot trefoil, ragwort, musk thistle and black mullein. A rare species, sickle medick, hybridizes freely with cultivated lucerne producing a wide range of variously coloured flowers from blackish purple to sulphur yellow. An unusual feature of Breckland is that normally pink or purple flowers appear as white varieties here – this occurs in heather, storksbill and wild thyme. Four plants found in Breckland but not elsewhere in Britain are: Spanish catchfly, field wormwood, spring speedwell and wild thyme.

Thorney, *Cambs,* the most northerly of the Fenland islands, a monastery was founded here in 657 but destroyed by the Danes in the following century. Thorney Abbey was refounded by the Benedictines in 972 and a 12th-century writer described it then as 'a little paradise, delightsome as Heaven itself may be deemed, fen-encircled, yet rich in lofty trees. And what of the glorious buildings, whose very size it is a wonder that the ground can support amid such marshes'. Alas, little remains of the glorious buildings now: they suffered at the Dissolution and only the tall west front and part of the nave survive.

Thorney has an unusually tidy look because the Bedford family own it and have created a model estate village, complete with well-planted trees. It was the Bedfords too who allowed Huguenot refugees to settle here in the 17th century; many of their graves survive in the churchyard, looking somehow sad, as all 'foreign' graves appear.

Windmill, Thorpeness

Thorpeness, *Suff,* is an odd place. Stuart Ogilvie, a friend of Henry Irving, bought most of the land there in the early 1900's and built a complete village in a mock-Tudor style. One of the most famous fantasies is the 'House in the Clouds', a water tower designed to look like a house (it stands on an 85-foot shaft). Nearby is a fine 19th-century windmill. It was moved from Aldringham not far away to add to the jollity of Mr Ogilvie's Thorpeness!

Tolleshunt D'Arcy, *Essex.* This splendidly-named village recalls the Tolleshunt and D'Arcy families, the latter living in the 15th-century hall. The hall has a square moat crossed by a bridge dated 1585. The church of St Nicholas has several interesting features including an octagonal font decorated with shields and rosettes, a collection of brasses mainly of the D'Arcy family – note particularly that to Thomas D'Arcy, his wife and their nine children.

Waltham Abbey, *Essex,* is famous in history and also in legend. The legend relates that a standard bearer of Canute called Tovi discovered a fragment of the Holy Cross in Devon and built a church here to house it. So much for the legend. We do know that Earl Harold, later King Harold rebuilt a church on the same site in 1060, and it is strongly believed that he was buried here after the Battle of Hastings. 300 years later Henry II founded a priory at Waltham which soon became an abbey of some importance. (He founded three monasteries in expiation for his murder of Thomas Becket). Excavation has shown in recent years that this abbey was 400 feet long with two central towers, each tower having transepts, those next to the choir being 140 feet wide. Henry VIII suppressed the abbey and most of it was demolished except for the nave and great gateway, now standing north of the church tower.

Today, we approach the church through the west doorway, 600 years old and refashioned somewhat when the west tower was rebuilt in 1558. Inside is the splendid Norman nave; the pillars, triforium and clerestory are decorated with typical Norman zigzag patterns, some of the columns having spirals cut in them which were once filled with gilt metal. The ceiling, however, is late Victorian and was painted by Sir Edward Poynter. Below the beautiful rose window are three windows designed by a colleague of Poynter, the Pre-Raphaelite painter Sir Edward Burne-Jones.

The monuments here include that of Sir Edward Denny, depicted with his wife and their ten children – he died in 1600; also of Lady Elizabeth Greville, the cousin of Lady Jane Grey.

The Lady chapel is entered from the south aisle – this is 14th century mainly, with particularly fine windows. Below the chapel is a crypt housing several local curios including the old Waltham stocks and whipping post (the latter oddly enough with ornate carving), a portrait of Thomas Tallis, who was organist here in the last days of the abbey, and casts of the abbey seals.

Wells-next-the-Sea, *Norf,* (Tour 8) is a small port and seaside resort. It has fine Georgian houses round the central green, called the Buttlands, and down on the quay there is a mixture of warehouses, cranes, shops and cafés. There are complaints that it is being uglified to attract popularity. Local boats land catches of sprats and whelks – in fact almost all the whelks sold in Britain come from Wells.

White Notley, *Essex,* is a pleasant village with some architectural surprises. The church has a Norman chancel containing Roman brickwork and a timber-framed belfry. There is also timber-framing in the 16th-century manor house and an old village lock-up dating from the early 19th century.

*****Wicken Fen Nature Reserve,** *Cambs,* (Tour 10) has been in the possession of the National Trust for 70 years and is an intriguing place to visit, showing what the Fenland used to be like. You can see sedge and reeds growing for use in thatching, peat cuttings and brickpits. Most people will be interested in the little pumping windmill (woodwork restored but ironwork original) which was rescued and brought to its present site to pump water up into the fen. The nature reserve is in fact some eight feet above the surrounding cultivated land and water must therefore be brought up to it. Wildflower enthusiasts will find here wild orchids, giant mare's tail, hart's tongue fern, water plantain, marsh pea, meadow-rue and meadow-sweet.

Although entry to the Fen is free, you should report your arrival to the information centre.

Willingham, *Cambs,* (Tour 12) has an interesting church with some really ancient parts. St Mary's stands on the site of a Norman church and there are carved stones from the Norman church in the west porch, one of the Norman columns contains traces of a Saxon coffin lid! The church tower is striking: tall, battlemented and pinnacled with a spire supported by crocketed flying buttresses. Inside, 14th-century arcades rise to a 15th-century clerestory and a marvellous hammerbeam roof with angels on the posts. Note also the medieval wall paintings and the unusual depiction of parrots on a red background on the parclose screens. Altogether a charming edifice.

****Wimpole Hall,** *Cambs,* (Tour 12) (NT) described as the largest house in Cambridgeshire, is renowned for the number of celebrated architects and landscape gardeners who have contributed to its appearance. The first house on the site was built in the 1640's, but only a few of its internal walls survive. It came into the 1st Earl of Hardwicke's possession in 1740 and remained with the family until 1894 when the convivial 5th Earl, more popularly known as 'Champagne Charlie', had to sell it to pay his debts. It was bought by Rudyard Kipling's daugher, Mrs Elsie Bambridge, in 1939. Her husband died in 1943, but she courageously spent the remaining thirty years of her life demolishing parts of the house and furnishing it in a suitable style. She left the house and 3 000 acres of land to the National Trust.

The Lord Chancellor's Room, Wimpole Hall

The tall central block of the house defines the size of the 17th-century original; the side wings were added in 1714, when the central block was refaced to match them. The entrance hall was modelled in the 1840's and now has florid Ionic columns contrasting with Soane's later Greek Revival columns in the background. The south drawing room, with its beautiful plasterwork ceiling, contains Italian painted furniture collected by Mrs Bambridge. The book room was designed by Soane, the furniture being Regency in style. It leads to the magnificent library, designed by James Gibbs; note the curious oak pulpit on castors to enable a reader to reach the upper bookshelves.

But the glory of Wimpole is Sir John Soane's Yellow Drawing Room. He made space for this by demolishing several older rooms and a staircase, giving him a space rising to the height of the house. Within this he designed a church-like room with a dome over a crossing, rather like a miniature St Pauls.

The baroque-style chapel was designed by James Gibbs and decorated by Thornhill.

The garden at Wimpole has been said to represent the history of English gardening from 1690 to 1830. It began with the creation of elaborate formal beds and canalized ponds, later to be 'naturalized' by Capability Brown in the 1770's and again by Humphrey Repton in the 1800's.

Wisbech, *Cambs,* (Tour 10) is surrounded by orchards and bulb fields and claims to be Capital of the Fens. Like so many other East Anglian towns, it was once nearer the sea than it is today – in fact it was built as a seaport. Situated on the River Nene, it has become an important trans-shipment centre again. You will see many European boats tied up at the riverside quays; barges also take loads up river to Peterborough. The town's prosperity was based on shipping in the 18th and 19th centuries and the lovely Georgian houses, built on either side of the river and known as the North and South Brinks, are clear evidence of commercial wealth. You may visit a splendid example in *Peckover House (NT) on the North Brink. It was built in 1772 and bought by Jonathan Peckover, founder of a local bank, at the end of the century. It contains much attractive carved wood and fine plasterwork. The garden is Victorian and has a number of rare trees including one of the largest maidenhairs in Britain – also orange trees under glass.

Wisbech's church of St Peter and St Paul has an unusual feature – twin naves and aisles; there is also a brass memorial, some seven feet long, to Sir Thomas de Braunstone. One of Wisbech's famous men was William Godwin, the 18th-century writer: his wife was that unusual woman Mary Wollstonecraft, and their daughter Mary married the poet Shelley and was the author of *Frankenstein*.

If you happen to visit Wisbech in the late spring you will be able to follow the marked routes which lead motorists through the blossoming orchards outside the town.

*The Wisbech and Fenland Museum, housed near the site of a Norman castle, contains many exhibits associated with Fenland life, as well as Roman and Celtic relics.

Witham, *Essex,* is a pleasant Georgian town, although its history goes back to the time of King Alfred, whose son built the defensive mound against the invading Danes. Nearby is the 14th-century St Nicholas church. If you take a stroll about Witham you will see many fine 16th-century houses and particularly the timber-framed Spread Eagle Inn. Down near the River Blackwater is the weatherboarded Blue Mills and other Georgian houses.

Tidal Mill, Woodbridge

Woodbridge, *Suff,* (Tour 2) stands at the head of the River Deben and, when boats were smaller, was an important port. It still remains a busy sailing centre and a place where yacht-building is a local industry. The town has many 18th-century buildings, and some Tudor: the Shire Hall on Market Hill was built in the 16th century and the Friends' Meeting House in 1678. The 15th-century St Mary's church has typical Suffolk flushwork of alternate knapped flint and freestone. Inside there is a rare Seven Sacraments font and a fine 15th-century screen. On the riverbank near the railway station you may see a tidal mill, said to be the last one in working condition in Britain. One of Woodbridge's famous men was Edward Fitzgerald, the translator of *The Rubaiyat of Omar Khayyam*: he used to entertain his writer friends at the Bull Hotel in the town.

Wroxham, *Norf,* (Tour 5) together with the adjoining Hoveton is regarded as the capital of the Broads and the intensive sailing and boat-building activity there in the summer is intriguing to watch. Roy's Stores in Wroxham, which provides for every need of the sailing fraternity, is said to be the biggest village stores in the world. Wroxham's church of St Mary, about a half a mile away from the bridge, is worth seeing if only for its south doorway, which is a fine example of late Norman decorative architecture.

Market Cross, Wymondham

Wymondham, *Norf,* (Tour 7) is a fascinating country town – it is pronounced 'Windham' by the way. The first feature you will notice is the market cross standing in the High Street: it is octagonal, standing on wooden arcades, and was built in 1618. Nearby is the Green Dragon Inn, a half-timbered building with interesting carving.

But the main attraction is the abbey church, unusual in that it has large towers at each end. The story behind this goes back to the foundation of a priory here by the Earl of Arundel around 1100, who intended the church to be shared by the priory and the townspeople. The monks and parishioners did not agree and the Pope decided that the nave, northwest tower and north aisle should be used by the people and the rest by the monks. This did not settle the quarrel and the monks walled off the nave from the choir of the church. The people then built the west tower in 1445. The monks then built the octagonal tower, originally in the middle of the church but now, because the monks' choir has now been destroyed, at the east end. The interior is lovely, the solid rounded Norman arches supporting a 15th-century clerestory and a breath-taking angel roof. Because of the extra tower there are no windows at the east end, but the modern reredos designed by Sir Ninian Comper is splendid.

12 Outstanding Motor Tours

The following pages contain 12 Tours which are felt best to convey the individual flavour of this part of Britain. Although varying slightly in mileage, any of them should be managed on a couple of gallons of petrol in the average family car. If you wish to cut short, or in other ways vary your route, the Tour Maps indicate where the Tour crosses or is part of the A road network. A separate map on pages 96 and 97 shows this network for the whole area.

The Highlights of each Tour are summarized on pages 98 and 99, and draw your attention to the major scenic or architectural places included in each Tour.

The directions given under each map have been set out so that the names of the places you pass through are given a new line, for easy reference. The mileage given after these place names refers to the total mileage from the previous place name.

If a place appears in **bold** type, you will find information about it in the alphabetical list in the Places of Interest section.

You will see that we have in many cases taken you along unclassified minor roads, indicated 'u/cl'. Although this will involve you or your co-driver in keeping a sharper look-out, it also leads to scenic delights you might otherwise miss.

Finally, for those who do not wish to keep rigorously to the routes shown, and in fact for everyone who feels that it is only sensible as well as more enjoyable to have a good map of the area, the up-to-date RAC Regional Map series will give you all the extra information you require.

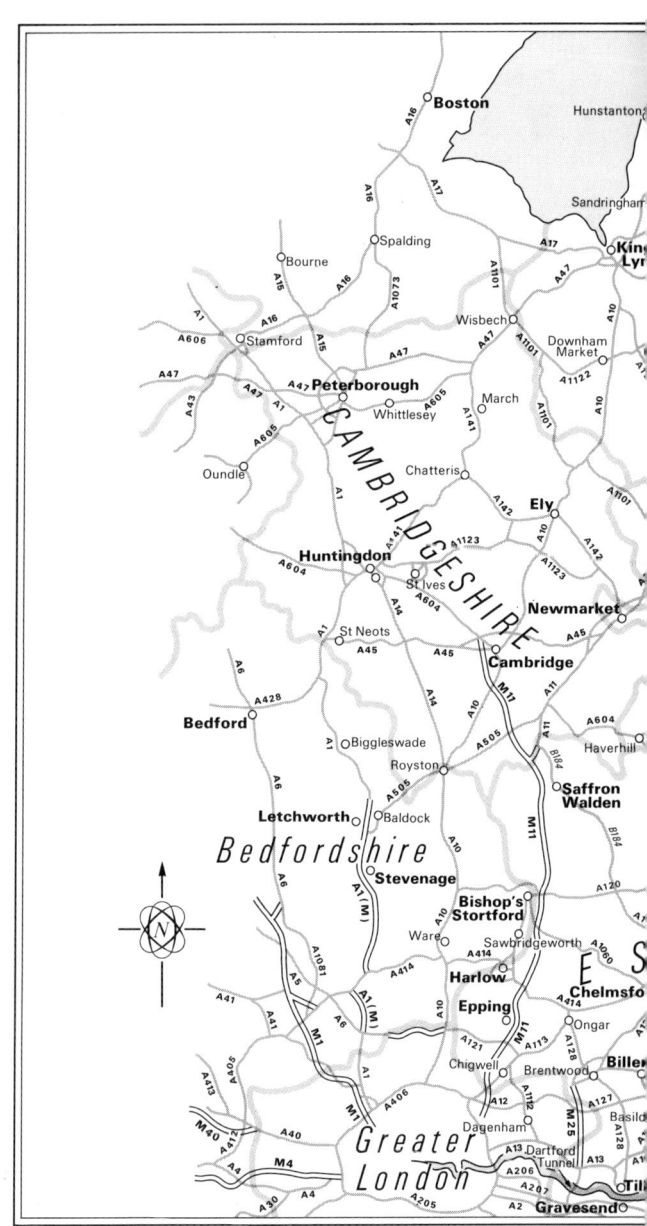

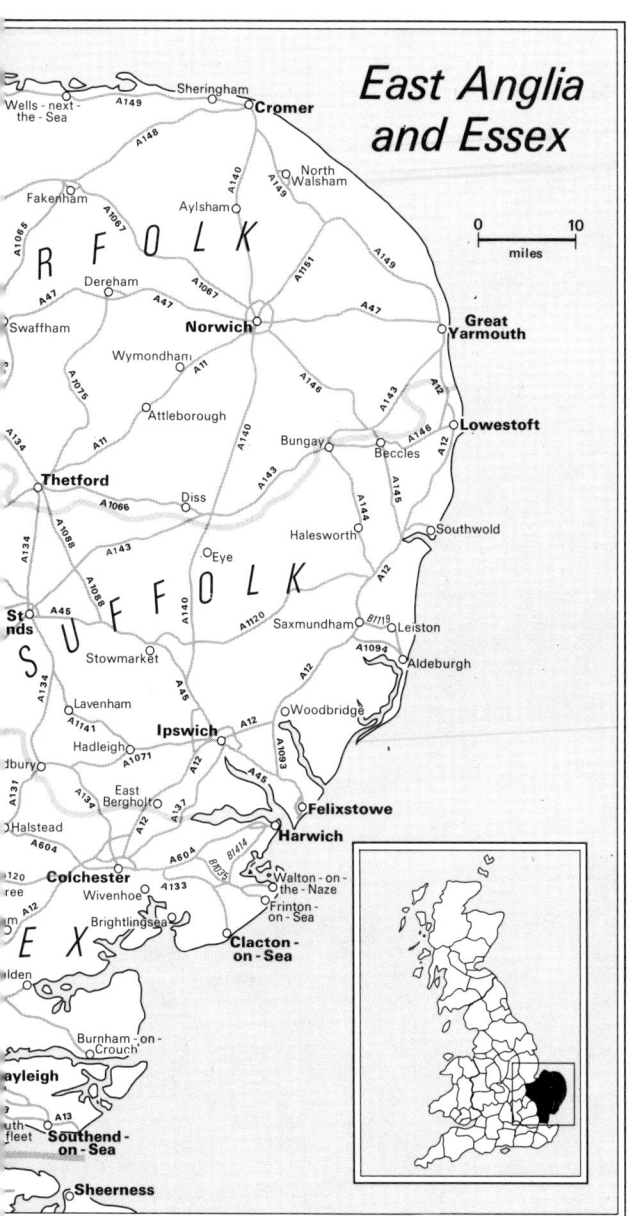

East Anglia and Essex

Highlights

Tour 1
Starting from Ipswich, you drive through Constable country, following the River Stour (birthplace of Gainsborough) to Flatford Mill, the background of *The Haywain*. The route includes Constable's birthplace at East Bergholt, and you may visit churches at Brantham and Nayland where he painted altarpieces. You also pass through the pleasant towns of Hadleigh and Bures, and pretty villages such as Hintlesham and Kersey. On the last few miles there are fine views over the Orwell Estuary.

Tour 2
From Ipswich, you go this time through the forests of Aldewood on to Aldeburgh and Snape, world-famous for the annual music festival started by the late Benjamin Britten. Two outstanding 12th-century castles can also be visited at Framlingham and Orford, the latter built to spite the Bigod family at Framlingham! Other places of particular interest are Woodbridge, at the head of the River Deben, Saxtead Green and Glemham Hall.

Tour 3
Of particular architectural interest on this tour are the 16th-century Layer Marney Towers gatehouse, Paycocke's House at Coggeshall, Bocking with its Tudor wool merchant's house, church and post windmill. The tour continues through hilly country to the remains of a great Norman castle at Castle Hedingham and the nearby church, also partly Norman. Finally, there is Little Maplestead where one of

the only five round churches in England can be seen.

Tour 4
You may enjoy comparing the similarities and differences between the fishing and seaside towns of Lowestoft and Great Yarmouth during this tour, the latter town containing some old merchants' houses similar to those seen at King's Lynn, perhaps stopping for lunch at the quiet seaside town of Southwold. The route also includes the Suffolk Wildlife Park at Kessingland. Part of the way follows the River Waveney from Beccles to Somerleyton Hall with its wealth of tapestries and paintings.

Tour 5
Blickling Hall, near Aylsham, is the first major attraction on this tour – a 17th-century mansion built in red brick and once the home of the Boleyns. Another house from the same period, Felbrigg Hall, may also be seen. Then you visit the seaside town of Cromer (which has a zoo) and for several miles down the coast road to Happisburgh. The return journey takes you through the heart of the Broads at Wroxham.

Tour 6
Two contrasting castles may be seen during this tour – Caister Castle built by Sir John Fastolf (Shakespeare's Falstaff) in the 15th century and the gigantic Burgh Castle, the best preserved of the Roman forts which once defended the East Coast against invaders. Also included are Great Yarmouth, with its many interesting features, the old town of Bungay and the unique Fair-

haven Garden Trust at South Walsham.

Tour 7
Wymondham, a charming market town, is the first attraction on this tour: it has an unusual octagonal market cross and a church, started in the 12th century, with two towers – the result of an ancient dispute between the townspeople and the monks of a former priory here. We also visit the Banham Motor Museum and Bressingham Gardens, famous for its three narrow-gauge railways. The return journey passes through Diss and Long Stratton.

Tour 8
Variety is the keynote of this tour, which includes Sandringham with its gardens; Castle Rising, a fine Norman relic; Castle Acre, the romantic ruins of a 15th-century priory; and Holkham Hall, a splendid Palladian house. Wells-next-the-Sea offers a pleasant place for a picnic beside the seaside.

Tour 9
This tour takes you through much of the huge Thetford Forest and is best enjoyed in good weather. Santon Downham, the administrative centre of the forest, is visited first. The tour then includes a visit to Grime's Graves, where, with white helmet provided, you may descend an ancient flint mine. To finish you can call at the beautiful moated Oxburgh Hall, still occupied by the family who built it 500 years ago.

Tour 10
Here is an opportunity to study the phenomenon of Fenland. Towards the beginning of the tour you visit Wicken Fen Nature Reserve, later calling in at Wisbech, 'the capital of the Fens'. The chief architectural interest lies in Ely Cathedral, begun in the 11th century, with a wooden lantern which still inspires awe and wonder.

Tour 11
Bury St Edmunds is a charming town with many attractions apart from the remains of the famous abbey. The route includes the dazzling Ickworth House, a neo-classical building with a high rotunda housing a unique collection of paintings, and Melford Hall, a 16th-century manor house. You also visit the highly-photogenic villages of Clare, Lavenham and Long Melford, the latter two with beautiful churches built during the 16th century, when these villages were rich from the wool trade.

Tour 12
A variety of pleasures are offered on this tour east of Cambridge. The main object is the newly opened National Trust property, Wimpole Hall, an 18th-century mansion formerly the home of Rudyard Kipling's daughter. Then there is Grantchester, the village near Cambridge associated with Rupert Brooke; Huntingdon, the birthplace of Cromwell (where you may visit the Cromwell Museum); St Neots, also with Cromwellian associations, and finally a quiet ride home through the orchard country north of Cambridge.

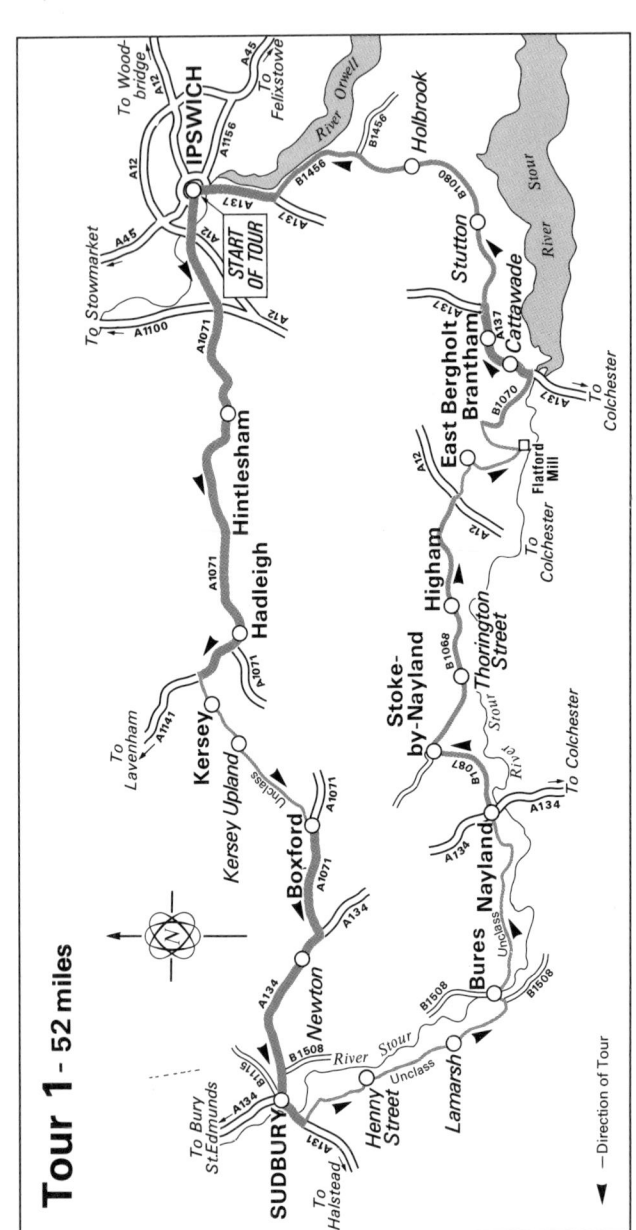

Tour 1 - 52 miles

IPSWICH

START OF TOUR

To Woodbridge

To Felixstowe

River Orwell

Holbrook

Stutton

Stour River

Cattawade

East Bergholt
Brantham

To Colchester

Flatford Mill

To Colchester

Higham

Stoke-by-Nayland

Thorington Street

Hintlesham

Hadleigh

To Lavenham

Kersey

Kersey Upland

Boxford

Nayland

Bures

To Colchester

Newton

To Bury St.Edmunds

SUDBURY

To Halstead

River Stour

Henny Street

Lamarsh

To Stowmarket

N

— Direction of Tour

100

Tour 1

Ipswich

Leave town centre following London A12 signs. In 1m turn R onto A1071 signed Hadleigh, to

Hintlesham 4m

Continue on A1071 to

Hadleigh 4½m

Turn sharp R at T-junction middle of town, in ¼m turn R on A1141 Lavenham road. In 1¼m turn L onto u/cl road signed

Kersey 2½m

Continue towards Boxford. At Kersey Upland 1m branch R then L. Turn R on reaching A1071, outskirts of

Boxford 3½m

Leave by A1071 signed Sudbury. In 3m turn R onto A134

Sudbury 6m

Leave by A131 crossing **River Stour**. In ¼m turn L into u/cl road for Bures. Keeping L after ¾m

Henny Street 2m.

Lamarsh 2m branch L to

Bures 1½m

Leave by u/cl road near church signed Nayland. In 4½m turn R on A134 then L on B1087

Nayland 5m

Leave by B1087 for

Stoke-by-Nayland 1½m

Turn R at X-road middle of village onto B1068.

Thorington Street 1¾m

Higham 1½m

Continue on B1068. In 2m turn sharp R and L crossing A12. Take u/cl road for

East Bergholt 3m

Turn R through village and by church R again, signed

Flatford Mill 1½m

Return along u/cl road. Turn R in ¼m. In ½m R again. In ¼m join B1070

Cattawade 2½m

Turn L onto A137 to

Brantham 1m

In ¾m turn R onto B1080

Stutton 2¼m

Here turn R and L

Holbrook 2m

In 1¾m branch L on B1456. In 2¼m turn R on A137 to

Ipswich 5¾m

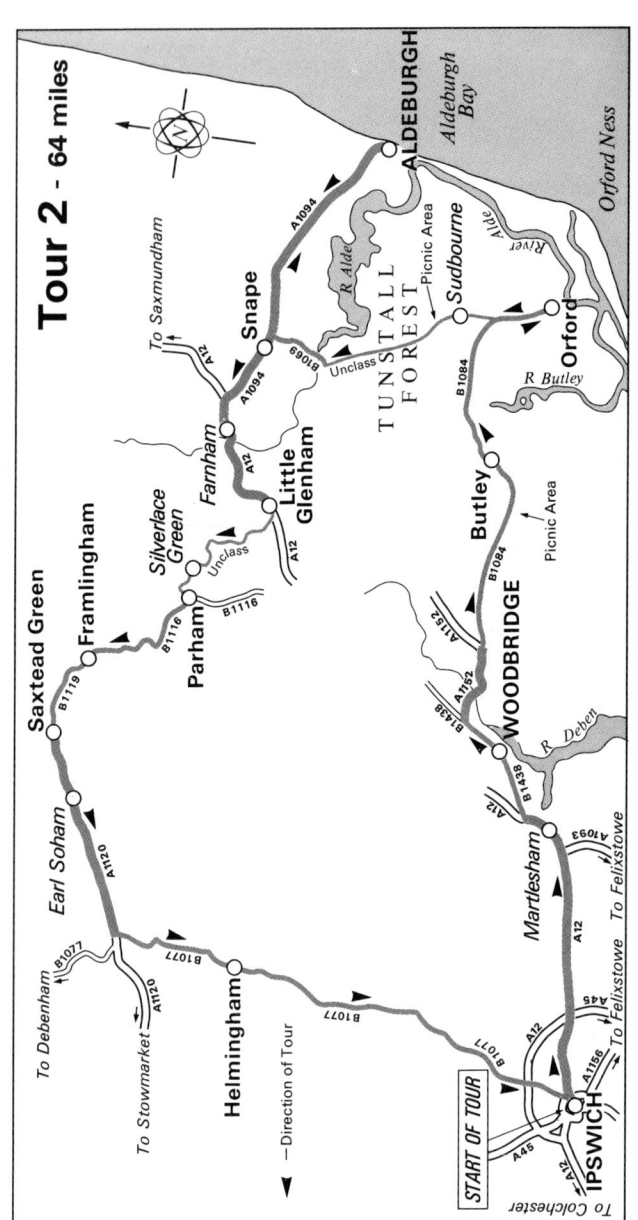

Tour 2 - 64 miles

N

ALDEBURGH

Aldeburgh Bay

Orford Ness

A1094

To Saxmundham

A12

Snape

B1069

R Alde

Picnic Area

Sudbourne

River Aide

A1094

Unclass

TUNSTALL FOREST

Orford

Farnham

A12

Little Glenham

B1084

R Butley

Silverlace Green

Unclass

Butley

Framlingham

B1116

Parham

B1084

Picnic Area

B1119

Saxtead Green

A1152

WOODBRIDGE

A1152

Earl Soham

A1120

B1438

R Deben

To Debenham

B1077

A1120

Helmingham

B1077

B1438

A12

Martlesham

A1093

To Stowmarket

B1077

To Felixstowe

— Direction of Tour

A12

To Felixstowe

A45

START OF TOUR

A1156

IPSWICH

To Colchester

A45

A12

102

Tour 2

Ipswich
Leave by the A12 signed Lowestoft
Martlesham 6m
In ½m turn R onto B1438 for
Woodbridge 1½m
Leave on B1438. In 1m fork R onto the A1152 signed Orford and after 1½m bear R onto B1084. In 3½m Butley Corner picnic site
Butley 7m
Continue along B1084 through
Chilsford 1m
Orford 3m

Retrace route on B1084 and in 1½m turn R on u/cl road signed Sudbourne and Snape. This goes through Tunstall Forest with a picnic site at Sangalls, 1m after Sudbourne. In 4m turn R onto B1069
Snape 7m
Turn R on A1094 to
Aldeburgh 5m
Retrace route to Snape. Then continue on A1094 for 2m to T-junction with A12. Turn L for Glemham Hall at
Little Glemham 9m

In ¾m turn R onto u/cl road. ¾m further turn R then ½m beyond turn L Silverlace Green 2m
Turn L for
Parham ½m
Turn R onto B1116 for
Framlingham 2m
Leave on B1119 to
Saxtead Green 2m
Turn L onto A1120 Stowmarket road
Earl Soham 2m
In 3m turn L onto B1077 for Ipswich
Helmingham 5m
Ipswich 9m

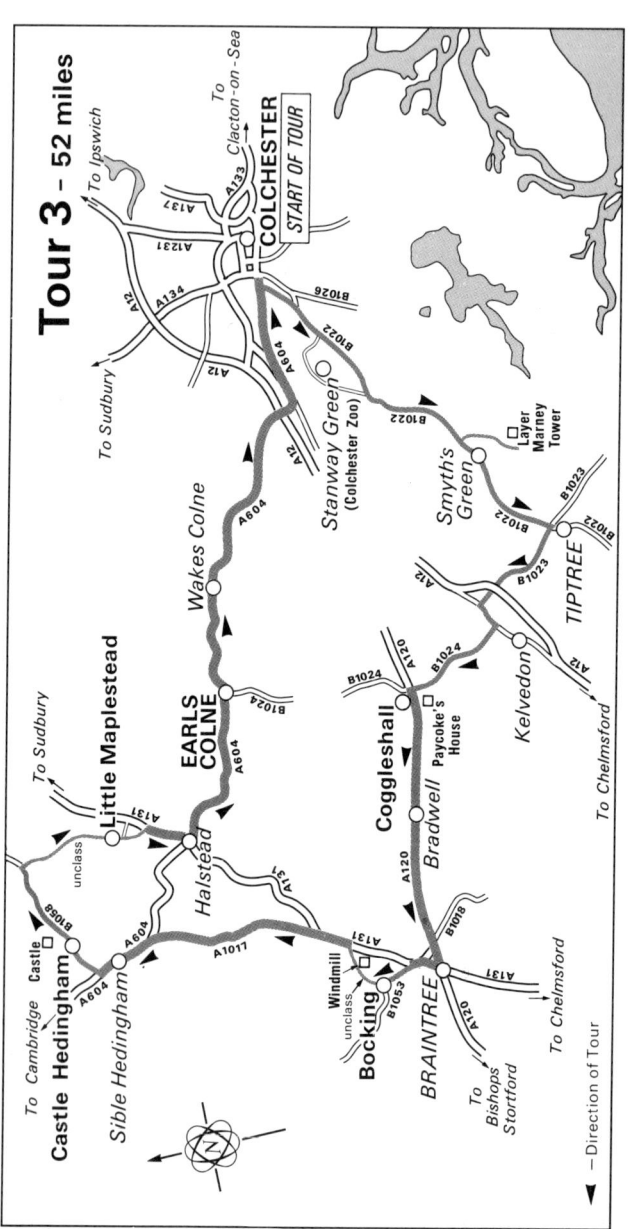

Tour 3 - 52 miles

To Ipswich
To Clacton-on-Sea
To Sudbury

A137
A12
A12
A131
A133
A134

COLCHESTER
START OF TOUR

B1026
A604
B1022

Stanway Green
(Colchester Zoo)

Smyth's Green

Layer Marney Tower

B1022
B1023

Wakes Colne

TIPTREE

B1023
B1022

A12

Kelvedon

B1024
A120

To Chelmsford

To Sudbury

Little Maplestead

EARLS COLNE

A604
A131

B1024

A604

Cogglestall

Paycoke's House

Halstead

A131

Bradwell

A120

To Cambridge

Castle

Castle Hedingham

B1058

A604

Sible Hedingham

A1017

A131

Windmill

unclass.

Bocking

B1053

BRAINTREE

B1018

A131

To Chelmsford

To Bishops Stortford

A120

To Chelmsford

N

— Direction of Tour

104

Tour 3

Colchester
Leave by A604 Cambridge road, turn L onto B1022 Maldon road for
Stanway Green (Colchester Zoo) 3m.
Continue along B1022, branch L in 1½m and then R after another 1½m to reach u/cl road L for
Layer Marney 4m
Follow markings, going straight over crossroads, then branch L to
Layer Marney Towers ½m
Retrace route to B1022 then turn L passing through Smyth's Green
Tiptree 4m
Turn R onto B1023 taking sharp R and L turn after 1m to reach A12 (underpass)

and then junction with B1024. Turn L here for ½m and then R on Station road (B1024) to
Coggeshall 5m
Turn L onto A120 (Paycocke's House is next to Fleece on L). Continue on A120 through Bradwell
Braintree 6m
Turn R onto A131, then L on B1053
Bocking 1m
Turn R opposite church on u/cl road then R again (Post windmill on R top of hill) then turn L on A131. After 1m branch L onto A1017. Turn L onto A604 Cambridge road
Sible Hedingham 6m

On outskirts turn R on B1058 for
Castle Hedingham 1m
Continue on B1058 taking third u/cl road on R, follow markings to
Little Maplestead 4m
Retrace road opposite church, turn R for A131 where turn R for
Halsted 2m
Turn L onto A604 for
Earl's Colne 3m
Wakes Colne 3m
Eight Ash Green 4m
At roundabout continue ahead and ¼m on turn L at a further roundabout, then keep R onto A1124 for
Colchester 5½m

105

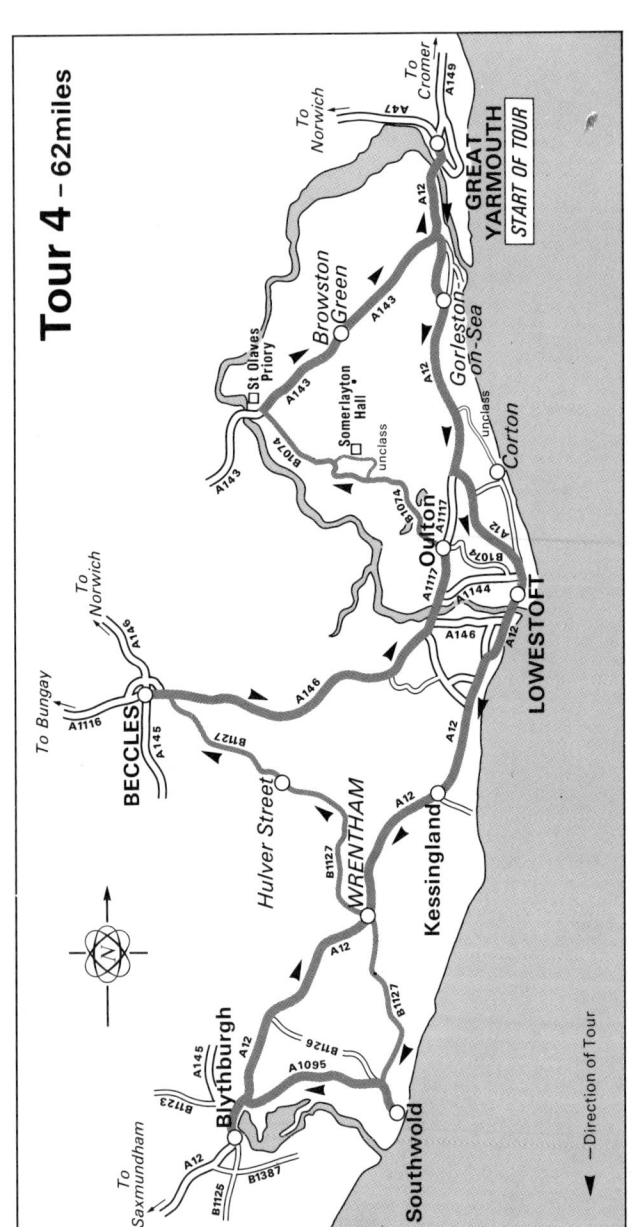

Tour 4 – 62 miles

GREAT YARMOUTH
START OF TOUR

To Cromer
A149
To Norwich
A47
A12

Browston Green
A143
St Olaves Priory
A143
A143

Gorleston on-Sea
A12
unclass
Corton
A12

Somerleyton Hall
unclass
B1074

Oulton
A1074
A1117
A1117
B1074

LOWESTOFT
A144
A146
A12

To Norwich
A149

To Bungay
A1116
BECCLES
A145
B1127

Hulver Street
B1127

WRENTHAM
A146
A12

Kessingland
A12
B1127

Blythburgh
A145
A12
B1123
B1126
A1095
B1127

Southwold

To Saxmundham
A12
B1125
B1387

N

— Direction of Tour

106

Tour 4

Great Yarmouth
Leave by A12 signed Lowestoft, passing through Gorleston on Sea, and reaching **Lowestoft** 10½m
Continue along the A12, marked to Ipswich, to
Kessingland 3½m
Continue along A12 for 4m and then fork L at Wrentham following B1127 to **Southwold** 8m
Return to outskirts of town, turn L onto A1095, to
Blythburgh 5m
Retrace route to north of town and take

the A12 to Wrentham 4m, where turn L onto B1127, passing through Hulver Street on way to
Beccles 14m
Leave by A146 for Lowestoft to Oulton Broad 7m
where follow A1117 to

Oulton 1m
Turn L onto B1074 for
Somerleyton Hall 4m
Continue along B1074 reaching T-junction with A143, where turn R, and so back to
Great Yarmouth 9m

Somerleyton Hall

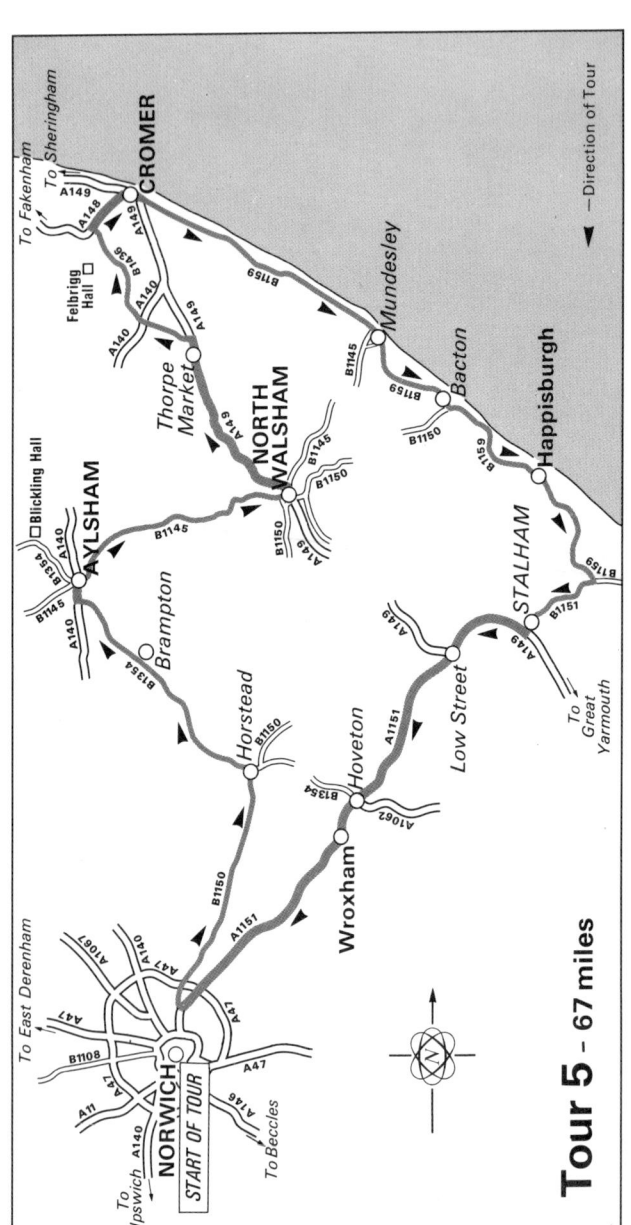

Tour 5 - 67 miles

← Direction of Tour

To Sheringham
To Fakenham
CROMER
A149
A148
A149
B1436
A149
A140
Felbrigg Hall □
B1159
Mundesley
Thorpe Market
A149
B1145
Bacton
B1159
Blickling Hall □
A140
B1354
AYLSHAM
NORTH WALSHAM
B1145
A149
B1150
B1145
B1150
Happisburgh
B1159
B1150
B1159
A140
B1145
Brampton
B1354
B1150
Horstead
A1151
Low Street
STALHAM
B1151
A149
A149
To Great Yarmouth
B1150
A1151
Hoveton
B1354
A1062
Wroxham
To East Derenham
A1067
A140
A47
A47
A47
A1151
A11
Ipswich A140
B1108
A140
A47
NORWICH
START OF TOUR
A146
To Beccles
To Ipswich
N

Tour 5

Norwich
Leave by B1150 reaching
Horstead 7m
Here turn R and L onto B1354 for
Aylsham 7m
Leave by continuation of B1354 north
side of Aylsham signed
Blickling Hall 1½m
Return to Aylsham then on the B1145 to
North Walsham 7½m
Leave by A149 Cromer road passing
through Thorpe Market and then fork L
on B1436 which crosses A140 to
Felbrigg Hall 9m
Continue along B1436 turning R at T-
junction with A148 and reaching
Cromer 2½m
Leave Cromer on coast road B1159
passing through Mundesley and Bacton
to
Happisburgh 14m
Continue south along B1159. After 3m
turn R onto B1151 signed
Stalham 5m
Leave by A149 turning R in Norwich
direction. After 2m where the road forks
R fork L on A1151 for Norwich reaching
Hoveton 6m
Wroxham 1m
Norwich 7m

Blickling Hall

109

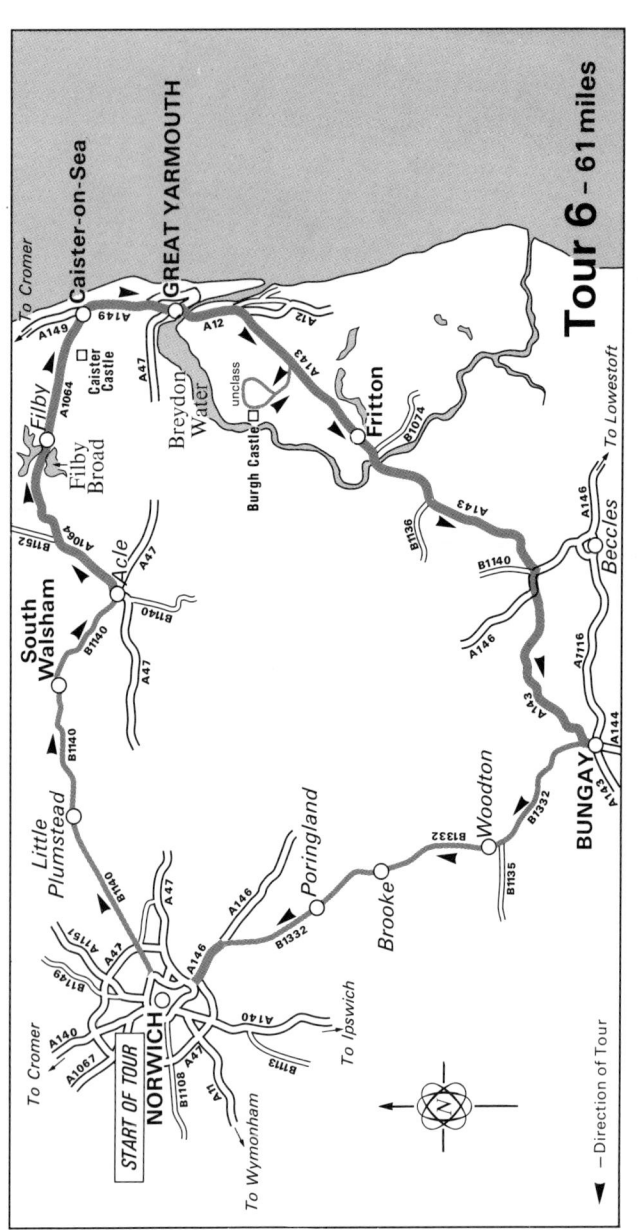

Tour 6 – 61 miles

To Cromer

Caister-on-Sea

GREAT YARMOUTH

A149
A149
A1064
Caister Castle
A47
Breydon Water
A12
A12
unclass
Burgh Castle
A143
Fritton
B1074

Filby
Filby Broad
B1152
A1064
Acle
A47
B1140
A47
South Walsham
B1140

B1136
B1140
A143
A146
Beccles
To Lowestoft
A7116

Little Plumstead
B1140
A47
A47
A1151
B1149
A140
To Cromer
A1067
NORWICH
START OF TOUR
B1108 A47
A11
To Wymondham
B1113
A140
To Ipswich
A146
A146
B1332
Poringland
Brooke
B1332
Woodton
B1135
B1332
BUNGAY
A143
A144
A144

N

▶ – Direction of Tour

Tour 6

Norwich
Leave by B1140 reaching
South Walsham 9m
Continue on B1140 to
Acle 3m
Fork L on A1064 Caister road to
Caister Castle 7½m
Continue on A1064 to
Caister-on-Sea 1m
Turn R onto A149 coast road to
Great Yarmouth 3m
Leave by A12 Lowestoft road bearing R
after 1½m onto A143 signed Bungay
reaching roundabout (note: White
Horse public house). Take u/cl Burgh
road signed
Burgh Castle 5m
Retrace road to A143 (do not be
tempted to try other roads!) where turn
R to
Fritton 5m
Continue along A143 cross A146 and
follow signs to
Bungay 13m
Retrace route to town outskirts and fork

L on B1332 passing
Woodton 4m
Brooke 4m
the B1332 forks L into A146 for
Norwich 7m

Butter Cross, Bungay

111

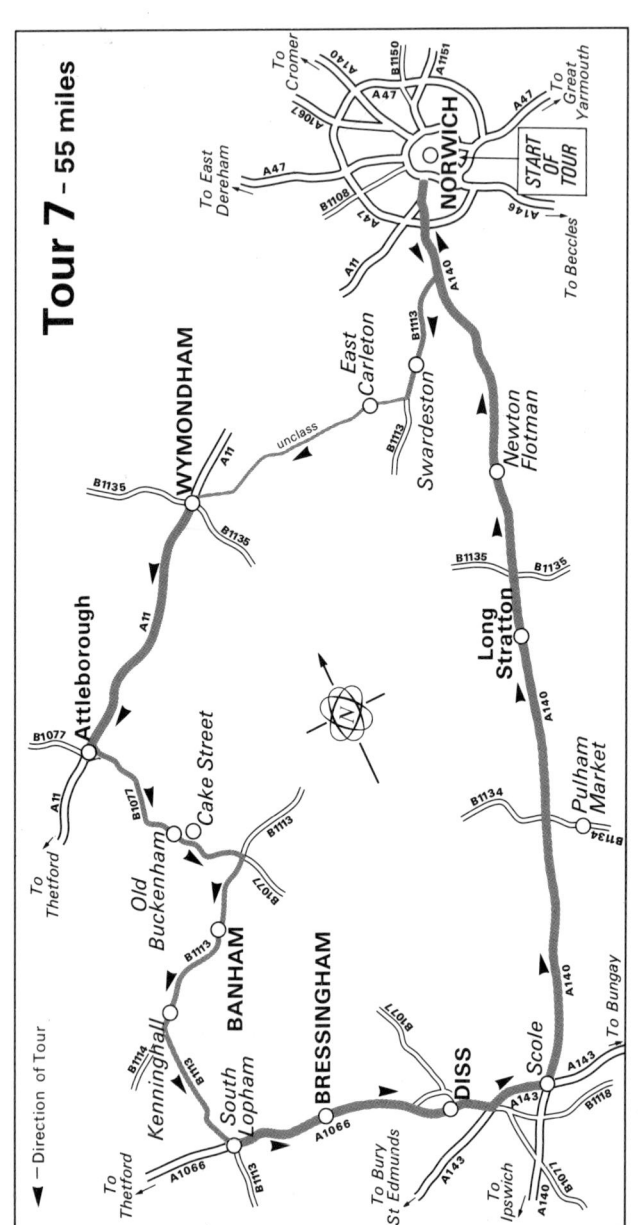

Tour 7 - 55 miles

← Direction of Tour

112

Tour 7

Norwich
Leave on A140 Diss road from near
Castle Museum, after 2½m fork R onto
B1113 passing
Swardeston 4m
In ¾m turn R onto u/cl road signed East
Carlton, passing through village and
forking L after church, to reach
Wymondham 6m
Leave by A11 signed Ipswich from near
Market Cross to
Attleborough 6m
Turn L onto B1077 branching R after
¼m and bearing R further ¼m, in 1m

turn L for
Old Buckenham 3m
In ½m turn L to
New Buckenham 1½m
At crossroads turn R onto B1113
Banham 1¾m
Keep R then L through Banham to
Kenninghall 2¼m
In ¼m fork L, still on B1113, for
South Lopham 3m
Here turn L onto A1066 reaching
Bressingham 2½m
Diss 3½m
Shortly keep L on A143

Scole 2m
Turn L onto A140 Norwich road
Long Stratton 9m
Newton Flotman 4m
Norwich 7m

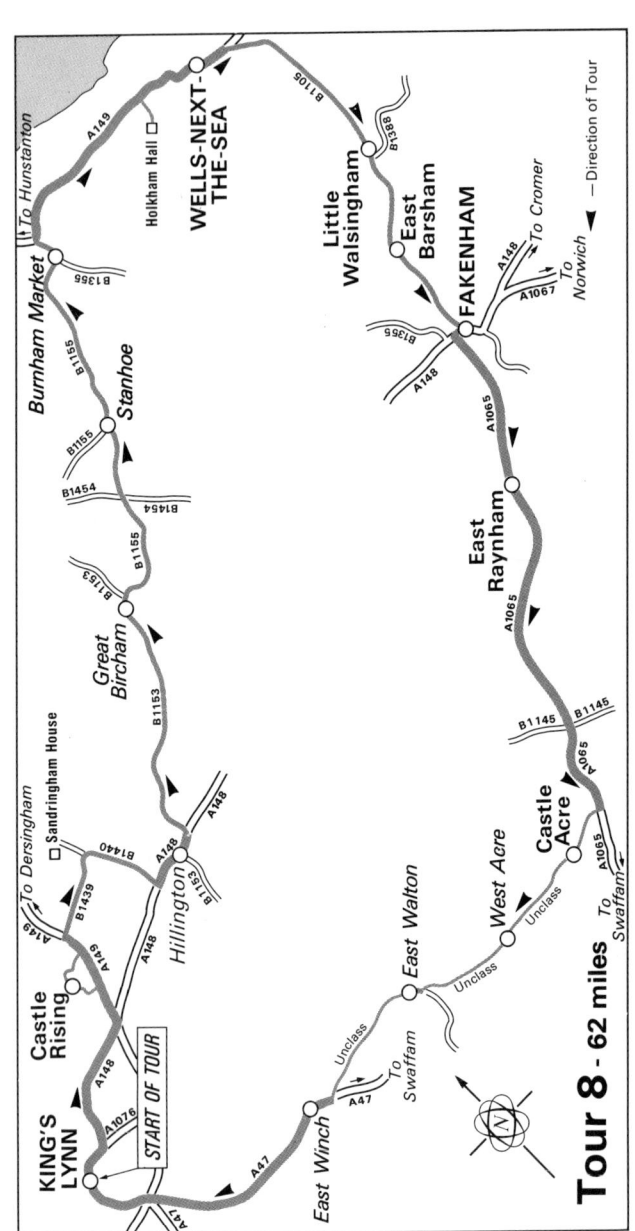

Tour 8 - 62 miles

KING'S LYNN
Castle Rising
To Dersingham
Sandringham House
Hillington
Great Bircham
Stanhoe
Burnham Market
To Hunstanton
Holkham Hall
WELLS-NEXT-THE-SEA
Little Walsingham
East Barsham
FAKENHAM
To Cromer
To Norwich
East Raynham
Castle Acre
West Acre
East Walton
To Swaffam
East Winch
To Swaffam

A149, A148, A1076, A47, B1439, B1440, B1153, B1155, B1454, B1355, B1105, B1388, A1065, B1145, A1067

START OF TOUR

— Direction of Tour

114

Tour 8

King's Lynn
Leave by A148 signed Cromer, turn L onto A149 signed Hunstanton
Castle Rising 4m
Continue along A149, turn R into B1439, (skirting **Sandringham Estate**)
Turn R onto B1440 to reach T-junction with A148, turn L for
Hillington 6m
In 1m turn L onto B1153 and continue through Flitcham to
Great Bircham 5m
Turn R and L onto B1155

Stanhoe 4m
Continue R on B1155 for
Burnham Market 4m
Turn L onto B1355 and R onto A149
Holkham Hall 3½m
Continue on A149 coast road to
Wells-next-the-Sea 2m
Leave by B1105 to
Little Walsingham 4m
East Barsham 2m
Fakenham 3m
Leave by A1065 signed Swaffham to
East Raynham 3m
Cross B1145, then turn R on u/cl road

signed
Castle Acre 8m
Leave on u/cl road at opposite end of village from priory signed
West Acre 2m
Then follow signed road to
East Walton 2m
Fork left here u/cl road, in 2m turn R on A47 for
East Winch 3m
King's Lynn 6m

Tour 9 - 62 miles

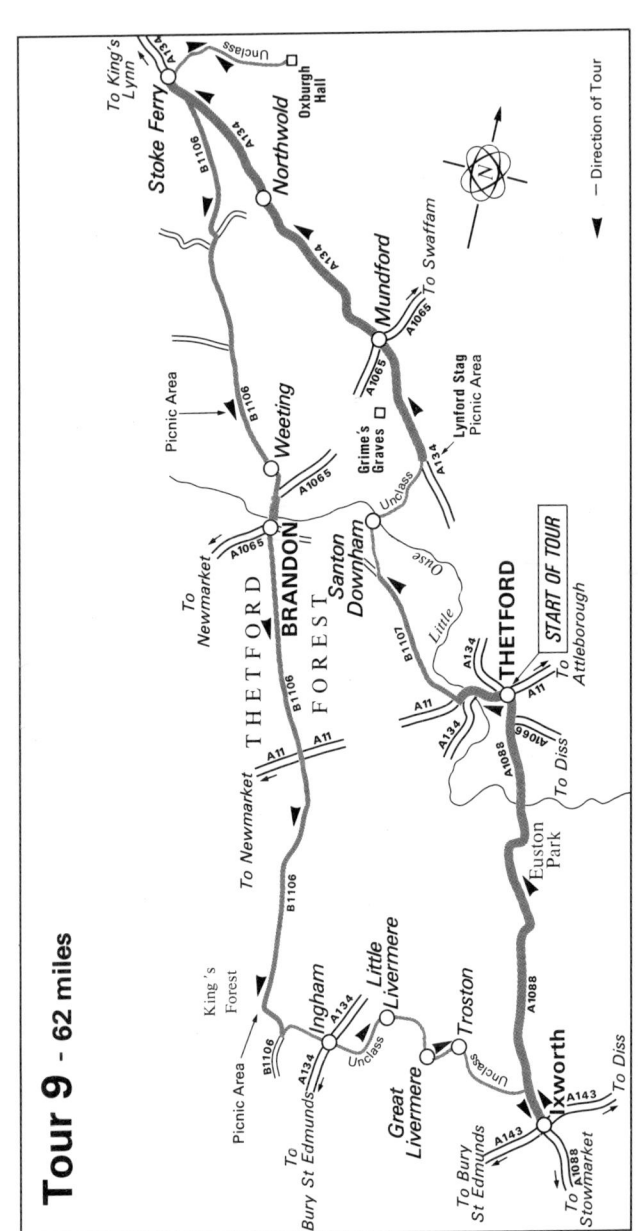

— Direction of Tour

Tour 9

Thetford
Leave by A11 Newmarket road and shortly turn R onto B1107 Brandon road. In 3½m turn R u/cl road for Thetford Forest Information Centre signed
Santon Downham 4½m
Continue downhill crossing Little Ouse river and in 1½m turn L onto A134 (Lynford Stag picnic site). Shortly turn L u/cl road signed
Grime's Graves 2½m
Continue on A134 crossing A1065
Mundford 2½m

(sharp R and L turn) through Northwold to
Stoke Ferry 8m
Turn R onto u/cl road signed
Oxburgh Hall 3m
Retrace route to A134, turn L. Shortly fork R onto B1106 for
Weeting 11½m
Fork R onto A1065 for
Brandon 1½m
Continue on B1106 for 9m crossing A11, to King's Forest picnic site. In 4m take u/cl road signed
Ingham 14m

Cross A134, follow signs to
Great Livermere 3m
Troston 1m
Turn R through village and on to A1088 where turn R for
Ixworth 3m
Return on A1088, continue to
Euston Park 4m
Continue on A1088 to join A1066
Thetford 2½m

117

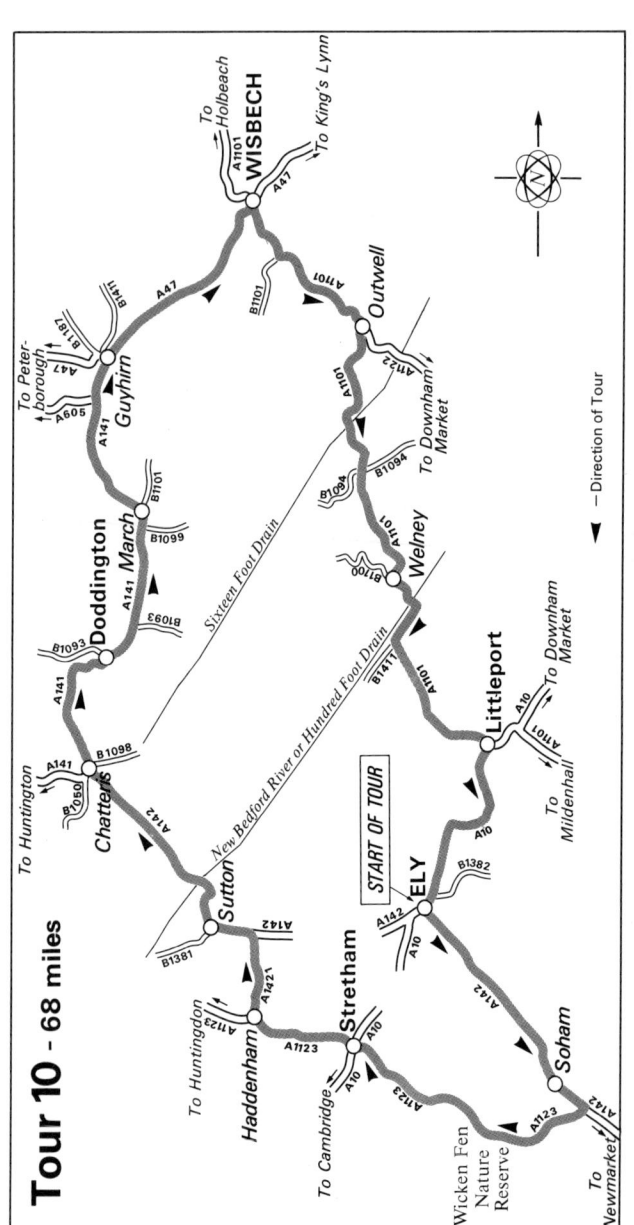

Tour 10 - 68 miles

Tour 10

Ely
Leave by the A142 Newmarket road
Soham 5m
Continue along A142 for 1½m then fork
R on A1123 Haddenham road to
Wicken Fen Nature Reserve 5m
Stretham 4m
Continue on A1123 turn R onto A1421
at
Haddenham 3m
Turn L at T-junction with A142
Sutton 3m
Continue along A142 to
Chatteris 6m

Leave by A141 for
Doddington 4m
Continue along A141 for 2¾m then take
the B1101 to
March 4m
Cross river and turn L on B1099. In 1m
return to A141 and at
Guyhirn 5m
fork R onto A47 Wisbech road
Wisbech 6m
Leave by A1101 Ely road, which forks R
at
Outwell 4m
and continues on to

Welney 7m
and
Littleport 6½m
Leave by A10 to
Ely 5½m

119

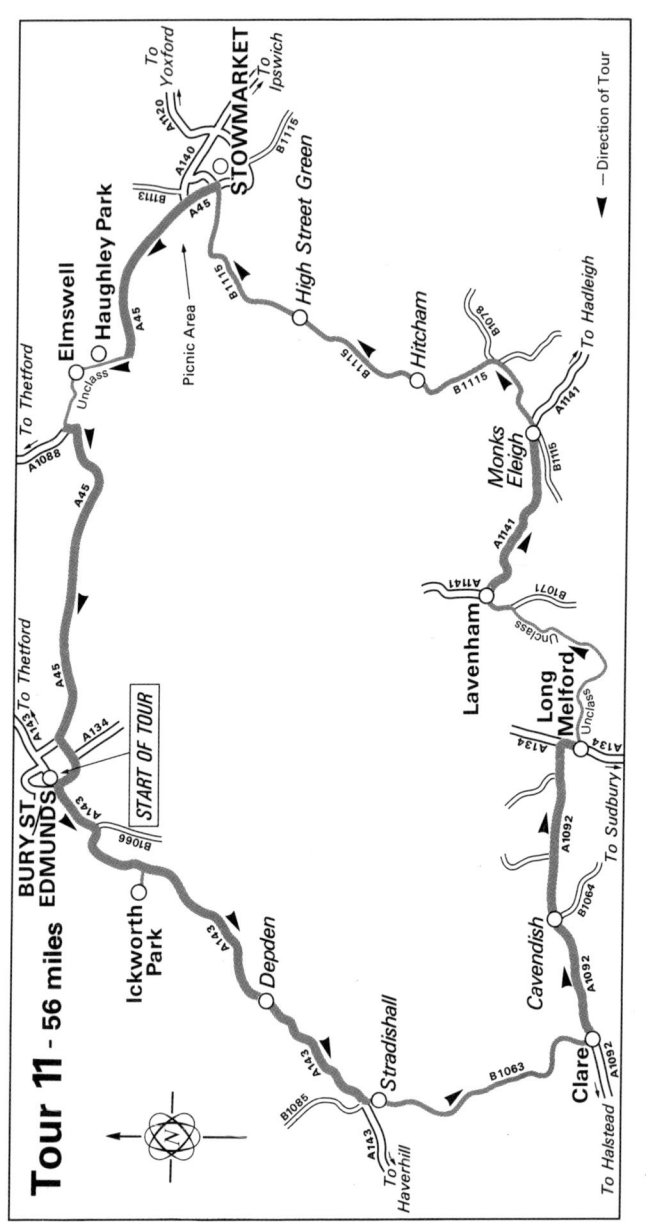

Tour 11 - 56 miles

- To Yoxford
- STOWMARKET
- To Ipswich
- High Street Green
- Haughley Park
- Elmswell
- Picnic Area
- Hitcham
- To Thetford
- To Hadleigh
- Monks Eleigh
- Lavenham
- To Thetford
- Long Melford
- BURY ST. EDMUNDS
- START OF TOUR
- To Sudbury
- Ickworth Park
- Depden
- Cavendish
- Clare
- Stradishall
- To Halstead
- To Haverhill

— Direction of Tour

Tour 11

Bury St Edmunds
Leave by A143 signed Haverhill
Ickworth House 4m
(The park is extensive and an excellent place for a picnic or walk). Return to A143, turn R
Stradishall 8m
Fork L here onto B1063 for
Clare 6m
Leave by the A1092 Sudbury road near the Bell Hotel to
Cavendish 2½m
Continue along A1092. Turn R at T-junction with A134 reaching

Long Melford 4m
Leave by u/cl road near Bull Inn signed Lavenham. In 1m fork L to
Lavenham 4m
Leave by A1141 signed Hadleigh; after passing through
Monks Eleigh 4m
branch L onto B1115 for
Hicham 4m
Great Finborough 5m
Stowmarket 2m
Leave by A45 signed Bury St Edmunds: in 2m, picnic place. In ¾m take u/cl road on R to

Haughley Park 3½m
Continue on u/cl road, turn R for Elmswell 1½m
then turn L and follow signs for Bury St Edmunds. Join A45 turn R for
Bury St Edmunds 9m

121

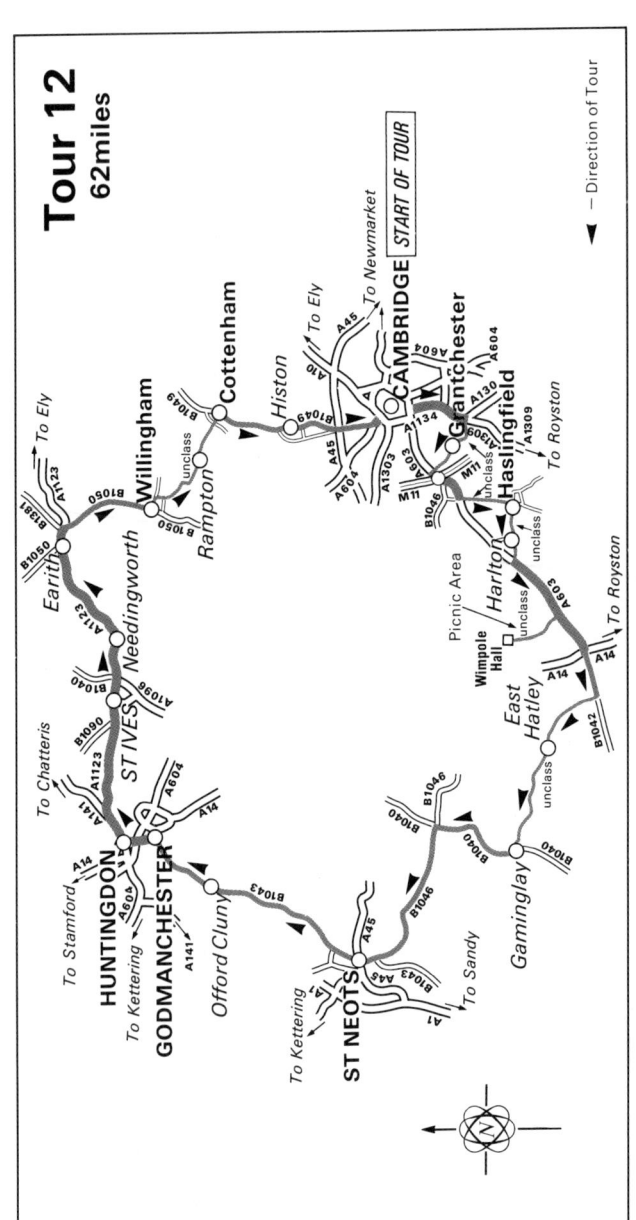

Tour 12
62miles

START OF TOUR

To Newmarket

CAMBRIDGE

To Ely

Cottenham

Histon

Willingham

Rampton

Grantchester

Haslingfield

Earith

Needingworth

Harlton

To Royston

ST IVES

Picnic Area

Wimpole Hall

East Hatley

Gamlingay

HUNTINGDON

GODMANCHESTER

Offord Cluny

ST NEOTS

To Chatteris

To Stamford

To Kettering

To Kettering

To Sandy

To Royston

▼ — Direction of Tour

N

Tour 12

Cambridge
Leave by London road A1134, keep R on A1309 and after 2m turn R at Trumpington on u/cl road marked to
Grantchester 3½m
Fork L after village and in 1m reach roundabout where turn L onto A603. After 1¼m turn L again onto u/cl road to
Haslingfield 4½m
Leave by u/cl road marked to Harlton 1¼m
Continue to A603 where turn L. In 2m turn R u/cl road signed

Wimpole Hall 3m
Return to A603 where turn R and after 1½m on meeting A14 turn sharp R and L onto B1042, turn R in 2m onto u/cl road to
Gamlingay 10m
Leave by B1040 marked St Neots. After 3m sharp L turn into B1046
St Neots 9m
Leave by B1043 for
Godmanchester 7m
Follow signposts to
Huntingdon 1m
Leave by A141, turn R into A1123

St Ives 5m
Earith 5m
and after ½m turn R on B1050 for
Willingham 3m
Leave by u/cl road near church marked to Rampton reaching
Cottenham 4m
Turn R on B1049 for Histon and then
Cambridge 6m

Opening Times of Important Places of Interest

The dates and times given were correct at the time of going to press. Unless am or pm are specifically shown, places are open throughout the day.

Banham Motor Museum *Easter – Oct; Suns only Oct – Mar*

Blickling Hall *Hall & garden: pm Wed Thu Sat Sun, Apr – Spring Hol; also 1-12 Oct; 11am Tue Wed Thu Sat, Spring Hol – end Sep, during which period garden only Mon & Fri*

Bressingham Garden & Steam Museum *pm May – Sep; also Sun and Thu; also Wed in Aug*

Bungay Castle *Daily*

Burgh Castle *Daily ex am Sun, Oct – Mar & Xmas Hols*

Bury St Edmund's: Clock Museum *Mon – Sat ex Bank Hols*
    Moyses Hall *Mon – Sat*

Caister Castle *May – Sep*

Cambridge: Colleges *Most are open daily, but notices state size of parties allowed*
    Botanic Garden *Mon – Sat; pm Sun*
    Fitzwilliam Museum *Tue Sat, pm Sun. Galleries never open all at one time*

Castle Acre Priory *See Burgh Castle*

Castle Rising *See Burgh Castle*

Coggeshall: Paycocke's *pm Wed Thu Sun, Apr – end Sep*

Colchester: Museum *Mon- Sat; also pm Sun, Apr – Sep*
    Zoo (Stanway Green) *Daily ex Xmas Day*

Cromer: Zoo *Daily*
Felbrigg Hall *pm Tue Wed Thu Sat Sun, Apr – mid Oct*

Framlingham Castle *See Burgh Castle*

Fritton Lake *Apr – end Oct*

Glemham Hall *pm Wed Sun & Bank Hol, mid Apr – end Sep*

Gosfield Hall *Wed Thu, May – end Sep*

Gt Yarmouth: No 4 South Quay *Mon – Fri; also Sun during Jun – Sep*

Hedingham Castle *pm Tue Thu Sat, May – Sep*

Haughley Park *pm Tue, May – end Sep*

Helmingham Hall Gardens *pm Sun, Jun – end Sep; also pm Wed, May – mid Sep*

Holkham Hall *Thu, Jun – Sep; also Mon, Jul – Aug*

Huntingdon: Cromwell Museum *Daily ex am Mon Sun & Bank Hols*

Ickworth House *pm Tue Wed Thu Sat Sun, Apr – mid Oct*

Ipswich: Ancient House *Mon – Sat ex Bank Hol*
    Christchurch Museum *Mon – Sat ex Bank Hol*
    Ipswich Museum & Art Gallery *Mon – Sat ex Bank Hol*

King's Lynn: St George's Guildhall *Mon – Fri; also am Sat*

Layer Marney Towers *pm Thu Sun, Apr – 1 Oct; also pm Tue, Jul – Aug*

Long Melford: Melford Hall *pm Wed Thu Sun, Apr – end Sep*

Norwich: Bridewell Museum *Mon – Sat ex Public Hol*
    Castle Museum *Daily ex am Sun & Bank Hol*
    St Peter Hungate Museum *Mon – Sat*
    Stranger's Hall Museum *Daily ex Sun & Bank Hol*

Orford Castle *See Burgh Castle*

Oxburgh Hall *pm Tue Wed Thu Sat Sun, Apr – mid Oct*

Sandringham Gardens *Tue Wed Thu, mid Apr – end Sep. Closed last week in Jul*

Somerleyton Hall *Thu Sun, Easter – end Sep; also Tue Wed, Jul – Aug*

South Walsham: Fairhaven Garden Trust *pm 2nd Sun, Apr – last Sun Sep; also pm Thu & Sat during that period; also Bank Hol*

Stanway Green: *see Colchester Zoo*

Stowmarket Museum of East Anglian Life *Mon – Sat; also pm Sun*
Suffolk Wildlife Country Park *Daily, Apr – Sep*

Thetford: Ancient House Museum *Mon – Sat; also pm Sun*

Wicken Fen *Daily*

Wimpole Hall *pm Tue Wed Thu Sat Sun, Apr – mid Oct*

Wisbech: Wisbech & Fenland Museum *Tue – Sat*
    Peckover House *pm Tue Wed Thu Sat Sun, Apr – mid Oct*

Index

This index does not include places with comprehensive information already listed alphabetically in the Places of Interest section, unless as a cross-reference to another part of the book

127

RAC Regional Atlas Navigator Series
● 1 South, Southeast, Thames & Chilterns, London ● 2 The
West Country, South Wales, Bristol, Cardiff ● 4 Northern
England: Lakes, Borders, Leeds, Manchester ● 3 The
Midlands (in preparation).
First ever atlases to be compiled from RAC local maps: scale
1.6 miles to 1 inch